BOULDER JUNCTION AREA
By Bob Knops

Research and Special Editing

Steve Brich and Russ Warye

Published by:
Fishing Hot Spots
Rhinelander, WI 54501

First Printing, 1977
Second Printing, 1979
Third Printing, 1983
Fourth Printing, 1985
Fifth Printing & Update, 1988
Sixth Printing & Second Update, 1991
Copyright ©, 1991
Fishing Hot Spots, Inc.
Rhinelander, WI 54501
ISBN 0-939314-04-5

Final Editing - Jay Christianson and Mark Martin
Drafting & Cartography - Bill Lambele
Word Processing - Tracy Jenkins
Electronic Layout - Jay Christianson

LAKES ALPHABETICALLY

Copies of "**Fishing Hot Spots: Boulder Junction Area**" and other books in the north central series may be obtained by writing:

Fishing Hot Spots, Inc.
1999 River Street
P.O. Box 1167
Rhinelander, WI 54501
or
Call Toll Free -- 1-800-338-5957

TABLE OF CONTENTS

BOULDER JUNCTION AREA SERVICE LISTING

● **THE BOOKWORM**
Complete line of Fishing Hot Spots and other fishing books, nature books, etc.
(715) 385-2191
Open Year-Round.
Downtown Boulder Junction

● **RICK'S AMOCO SERVICE**
Amoco products, batteries, live bait, ice, convenience items, tackle, Fishing Hot Spots Books.
(715) 385-2582
Open 7 days a week.
Downtown Boulder Junction

● **NORTHERN HIGHLAND SPORTS**
Complete fishing equipment, live bait, lake maps, souvenir T-shirts.
Jim & Carol Ashley
Box 67, Boulder Junction, 54512.
Downtown Boulder Junction

● **CAMP HOLIDAY, INC.**
Complete RV and tent camping resort.
Box 6, Boulder Junction, 54512.
(715) 385-2264
Rudolph Lake

● **BOULDER JCT. MOTOR LODGE**
New 20 unit motel, hot tub, in-room whirlpools, walking distance to res-taurants, continental breakfasts.
No pets, please.
(715) 385-2825
Downtown Boulder Junction

● **A-FRAME RETREAT**
Modern riverfront home w/boat.
100 yds. from Boulder Lake.
Spring/Fall Fisherman's Rate.
(715) 385-2056.
Manitowish River/Boulder Lake

● **HOMESTEAD TRADING POST**
"Look for the flying fish."
Fish decoys, carvings, fishing maps & books, gifts & furniture.
(715) 385-2428
Corner of Hwy M & High Lake Rd, ½ mile north of town.
Open Year-Round.

● **GEORGE'S STEAK HOUSE & MUSKYLOUNGE**
Fine dining, cocktails and lunches.
(715) 385-2350.
Downtown Boulder Junction

● **RUFFED GROUSE RESTAURANT**
Breakfast, lunch, full local line of Fishing Hot Spots maps & books.
(715) 385-2250.
Downtown Boulder Junction

● **J & S SPORTS**
Bait, tackle, Fishing Hot Spots maps & books, convenience items, gas.
(715) 356-7836.
On Hwy. N, ½ mile east of M/N intersection.

TRAVEL INFORMATION

WISCONSIN DIVISION OF TOURISM DEVELOPMENT 1-800-372-2737
Boulder Junction Chamber of Commerce .... (715) 385-2400

5

PREFACE

Extensive research has gone into the compilation of data in this Fishing Hot Spots book. Factual information was gathered from the Wisconsin Department of Natural Resources, local guides, area residents and field researchers.

Our goal is to provide information for successful fishing. Each Fishing Hot Spots lake report gives a complete profile of the body of water in an easy-to-use outline form. With technical information categorized into a quick reference format, our books will show you where to fish and what kinds of fish are available.

The outline form, which is standard to all Fishing Hot Spots publications, is briefly described as follows:

ACCESS - The location, types and features of lake access sites are described in the text and labeled on the survey maps. We have tried to give up-to-date information on every lake featured in this book, often through personal visitation to the sites by the Fishing Hot Spots staff. To avoid repetition, an access classification chart is shown below.

LAKE CHARACTERISTICS - The size and depth of the lake, water source, shoreline information, bottom composition, water clarity and fertility, oxygen levels and the types and amounts of vegetation are described.

Shoreline information is important because it often reflects the nature of the adjacent lake bottom. If the shore is wetland, then the lake will likely be shallow and weedy in that area.

Bottom composition refers to the type of material on the lake's floor. The different materials of muck, sand, gravel and rubble will influence what species of fish can naturally reproduce in a lake. Some species require gravel spawning habitat, some sand and others the matted vegetation of a muck bottom. Bottom composition will also affect the abundance and variety of the lake's food supply.

Water fertility influences fish productivity. An infertile lake may not sustain a reasonable fish community due to a limited forage base. If it is extremely fertile, an imbalance could be created where excessive weed growth poses the threat of winterkill or where pollution creates poor water quality best suited for rough fish. A lake in proper balance is able to sustain a fishery characterized by desirable size fish, good growth rates and levels of natural reproduction sufficient to maintain gamefish populations without stocking.

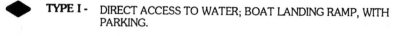

TYPE I - DIRECT ACCESS TO WATER; BOAT LANDING RAMP, WITH PARKING.

TYPE II - DIRECT ACCESS TO WATER; BOAT LANDING RAMP, WITHOUT PARKING

TYPE III - UNIMPROVED OR DIFFICULT ACCESS; ANY TYPE ROAD WITHIN 200 FEET OF SHORE, BUT NO DIRECT ACCESS TO WATER.

TYPE IV - WILDERNESS ACCESS; NO ROADS WITHIN 200 FEET OF SHORE.

TYPE V - NAVIGABLE WATER ACCESS; NO LAND ACCESS, BUT ACCESS BY BOAT FROM ANOTHER LAKE OR RIVER.

LAKE MANAGEMENT - Lake investigation data (such as netting study results) and stocking data are given on appropriate lakes. This section provides important information on the abundance and sizes of fish that are available based on fishery surveys.

FISHERY - A listing of what species of fish are present on each lake is provided. Usually, the various species are rated as primary, secondary or limited to indicate their relative abundance. Primary species are the most common, limited the least common. Species of fish listed in parenthesis indicates presence in extremely limited numbers, if at all.

RELATED SERVICES - Information on the availability of campgrounds, resorts, boat rental, bait shops, public parks and other services is supplied.

Featured in this book are lake survey maps. Unique to Fishing Hot Spots maps are shaded fishing areas that are accompanied by a description of each area in the text. These fishing areas tell anglers where, when and how to fish a particular lake.

The survey maps show lake bottom contours, an important characteristic to consider when you decide where to fish. Contour lines are roughly parallel to each other and represent an indicated depth of water. Additionally, contour lines show the size, shape and location of the various structures within a lake such as islands, humps, bars and holes. The edges of these structures are often key fishing areas.

Following is a Fishing Hot Spots map guide and legend. A review of this guide will enable you to quickly read the lake survey maps in this book and all other Fishing Hot Spots lake map/reports.

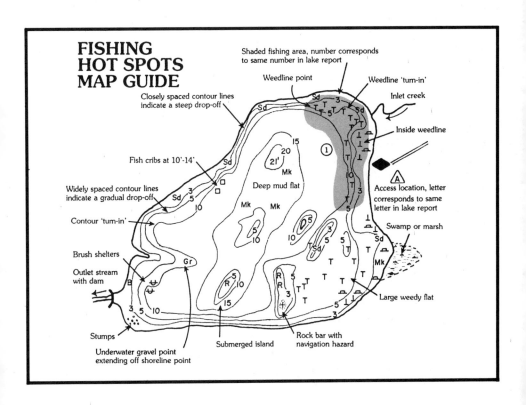

INTRODUCTION TO THE
BOULDER JUNCTION AREA

This well-known fishing area includes the popular vacation community of Boulder Junction. The area covers 124 square miles and includes 64 named and several unnamed lakes. Many of the more popular lakes are discussed in considerable detail, including Trout, High, Wildcat, Fishtrap, Big Muskellunge and Allequash.

In the Boulder Junction area, a place that calls itself "the Musky Capitol of the World," there is a wide variety of lakes offering diverse fishing opportunities. Many of the lakes are clear water lakes with a very high percentage of public access. In fact, only four of the lakes discussed in the book don't have some type of public access.

The region has tremendous public use facilities, with more than 80 percent of the 124 square miles in public ownership. There are also fine wilderness lakes, especially in the southern portion. Some of these waters are under special state management. Many of the lakes receive light to moderate pressure while some are heavily fished.

Although there are few major highways serving this large area, a number of paved and very scenic county highways network the lakes. U.S. Highway 51 borders the area on the west and brings anglers into Boulder Junction. County Highway M serves as the main access to many of the lakes and the town. Additionally, County Highways K, B and N extend in an east-west direction across much of the section.

A variety of fishing related services are available in the town of Boulder Junction. There are approximately a half-dozen live bait dealers, several tackle shops, sporting goods dealers, guide services, boat and motor repair, and rental services offered in town. Even though the town is small, it offers a nice northwoods atmosphere, yet it provides many recreational services.

There are many licensed guides in the Boulder Junction area. They are typically available any day of the week. Guides usually charge by the half and full day. Advance reservations are recommended, particularly in June and July. Ask locally or check with the Chamber of Commerce, the Guide's Association, resorts, campgrounds and bait and tackle dealers. Most competent guides will try to answer your questions and will serve as fishing instructors. Boat rentals are available on some of the lakes or in town.

Lodging is available on many of the larger lakes at a variety of resorts and motels. Camping is available at excellent private facilities and the campgrounds in the Northern Highland State Forest. Additionally, primitive canoe tripping campsites are located in the area, especially on the Manitowish River system.

As you will notice, the discussion of the individual lakes is not done on an alphabetical basis. The lakes are grouped geographically as shown on the section maps. An alphabetical listing is in the front of the book.

BOULDER JUNCTION AREA MAP

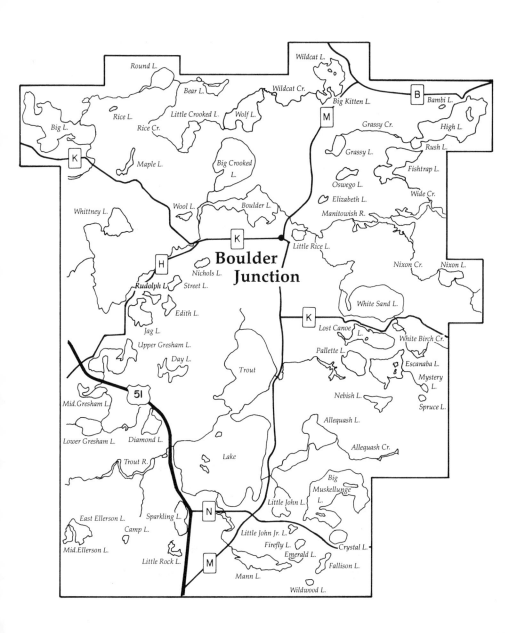

SECTION 1

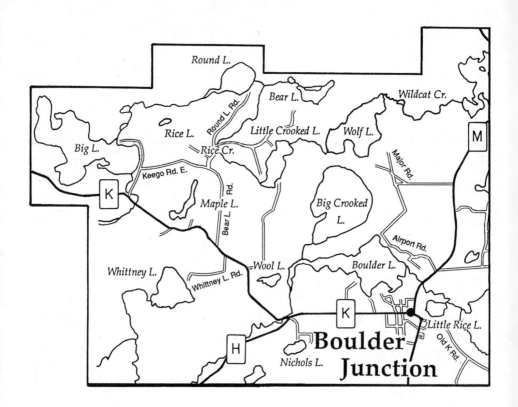

Big Lake	**Little Crooked Lake**
Round Lake	**Big Crooked Lake**
Bear Lake	**Whitney Lake**
Rice Lake	**Wool Lake**
Wolf Lake	**Boulder Lake**
Maple Lake	**Little Rice Lake**

BIG LAKE

LOCATION - In the northwest part of the book area, just north of Highway K and east of Highway P.

ACCESS

⚠️**A** **Type I (Public):** On the south side of the lake; from about 2 miles east of the intersection of Highways K and P, turn north from Highway K on the access road labeled "Big Lake Boat Landing." This state-owned facility includes a paved parking lot, turn-around, loading pier and a concrete slab ramp. The landing is fairly shallow but it is the best on the lake.

⚠️**B** **Type II (Public):** On the west end of the lake; take Highway P north of Highway K for 1.2 miles to the state forest campground. Turn east and proceed through the campground to the boat landing on the left. A paved ramp, turn-around and roadside parking are provided. The beach landing is shallow and is not suitable for larger boats.

Type V: Navigable access through the Rice Creek inlet and outlet.

RELATED SERVICES
Boat Rentals - None.
Resorts - None.
Public Parks - Yes, a small picnic area on the south side at Access A and at the state campground.
Campgrounds - Yes, a state facility on the northwest side of the lake.
Guide Services - Yes, in the area.

SPECIAL FEATURES - Big Lake is an excellent fishery and one of the premier lakes of Northern Wisconsin. An experimental, 40-inch muskie size limit is presently in effect.

LAKE CHARACTERISTICS
Size and Depth - 835 acres and 61 feet.
Water Source - Drainage lake: Rice Creek inlets on the north side from Round Lake, and an unnamed creek inlets at the northwest end. The Rice Creek outlet to Island Lake is at the southeast corner.
Shoreline - 44% state-owned, mostly along the east, south and northwest shorelines. 75% upland.
Bottom - 40% sand, 40% gravel, 20% muck.
Water - Fairly clear and extremely fertile.
Vegetation - Moderate densities of submergent and emergent species are present, especially on the west end, northwest side and the Rice Creek inlet. Cabbage and coontail are the primary submergent species.

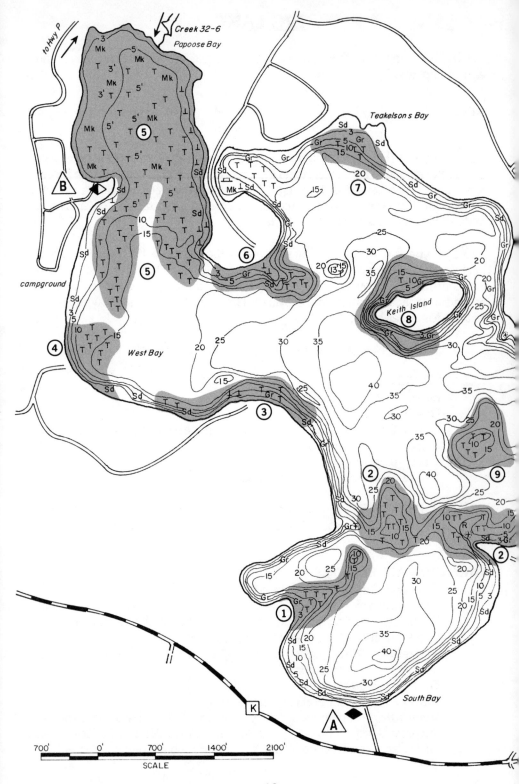

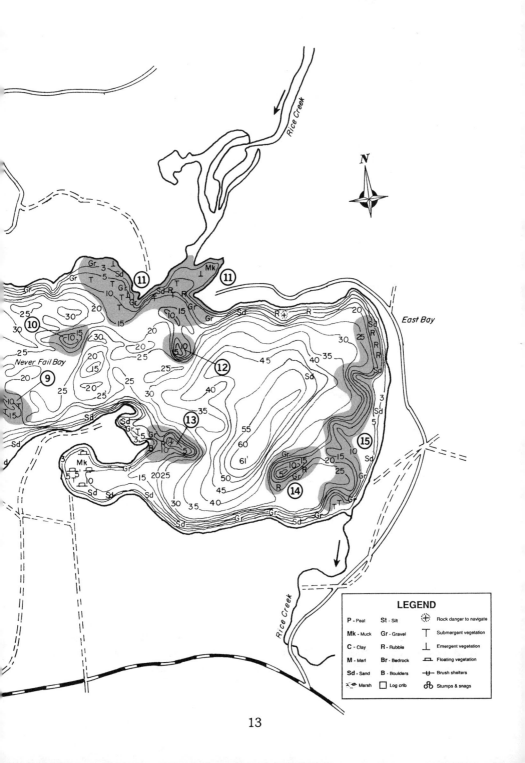

BIG LAKE

FISHERY

SPECIES

Primary - Walleye, Perch.
Secondary - Muskie, Largemouth Bass, Crappie, Rock Bass.
Limited - Smallmouth Bass, Northern Pike, Bluegill.

COMMENT - Muskie and walleye are the dominant predators and exhibit excellent growth rates. The size structure for both species is stable. Both bass species are self-sustaining, although largemouth are more numerous.
FORAGE - Minnows, shiners and juvenile panfish provide an adequate forage base. Rusty crayfish are present.

LAKE MANAGEMENT

Lake Investigation Data - A spring fyke net survey was recently conducted by the Wisconsin Department of Natural Resources to determine walleye and muskie abundance.

BIG LAKE FYKE NET SURVEY SUMMARY		
SPECIES	**SIZE RANGE**	**NUMBER**
Walleye	10" - 11.9"	215
Walleye	12" - 14.9"	485
Walleye	15" - 19.9"	118
Walleye	20" - 30"	50
Muskie	Less Than 31.9"	64
Muskie	32" - 42+"	139

The survey results indicated that adult walleye are fairly abundant, with approximately 3.3 fish per acre. Several strong year classes are present, and growth rates were average for this area.

A good population of muskie exist with many fish over 30 inches.

Stocking

BIG LAKE STOCKING SUMMARY			
YEAR	SPECIES	NUMBER	SIZE
1986	Muskie	1,700	8"
1988	Muskie	2,450	8"
1990	Muskie	2,300	Fingerling

LAKE SURVEY MAP - Fishing Areas Shaded

Area (1) During spring, crappie move toward the shallow cover found near shore. Slip bobbers and small fathead minnows are preferred at this time. Walleye relate both to weed growth and steep drop-offs year-round. When the cabbage and coontail beds become fully developed, anglers take muskie on bucktails or jerkbaits.
Area (2) Walleye and muskie are attracted to these underwater bars. Fish the weed edges for best results. The inside turns of the weedline tend to hold fish during cold front conditions.

Area (3) The submergent weeds along this steep drop-off yield both walleye and muskie. Backtroll this area in late summer and fall with live bait presentations.

Area (4) Spring walleye are taken from the developing weeds with 1/16 or 1/8 jig /minnow combos. Muskie are also present.

Area (5) This extensive region of submerged weeds provides excellent habitat for muskie, northern pike, walleye, crappie and largemouth bass. The deep weedline holds walleye, while muskie and northern can be found throughout the weedbed. Key on this area for early season muskie.

Area (6) Walleye use this weedy underwater point.

Area (7) Submergent weeds and sharp structure breaks combine to provide favorable habitat for walleye, muskie and panfish.

Area (8) Cast deep-diving crankbaits along the steep drop-offs surrounding Keith Island for summer and fall muskie.

Area (9) These underwater humps have submergent weed growth that attracts walleye in low light conditions. Muskie can also be present.

Area (10) Muskie are taken from this small underwater island on in-line spinners and naturally colored jerkbaits.

Area (11) Submergent and emergent weeds attract muskie, walleye, northern pike and largemouth bass to the Rice Creek inlet.

Area (12) Walleye and muskie use this small midlake hump during summer and fall.

Area (13) This shallow rock bar has yielded an occasional muskie. Use caution when boating in this area.

Area (14) Walleye and smallmouth bass frequent this rocky underwater island.

Area (15) The east shoreline features a number of sharp rocky breaks that hold summer walleye. The skillful use of a depthfinder is needed to locate and effectively work the underwater points and inside turns.

FISHING TIPS - Structure is the key to success on this top-notch lake. A depthfinder is necessary to locate deep weedlines, drop-offs and midlake structure.

Use standard walleye jig/minnow combinations in May and again from mid-September to ice-up. Leeches are the preferred bait during summer.

Muskie anglers should try black or brown bucktails with bright blades or brightly colored jerkbaits and crankbaits. In general, larger muskie tend to relate to midlake structure by early summer. Night fishing is also suggested, but shallow rock bars can hinder safe navigation.

CONCLUSION - Big Lake is one of the finest fishing waters of Northern Wisconsin. Both the fishery and the scenery are excellent, and trophy potential exists for both muskie and walleye.

ROUND LAKE

LOCATION - In the northwest part of the area, north of Highway K and west of Highway M.

ACCESS - Type I (Public): On the south side of the lake; take Bear Lake Road north of Highway K for 1.9 miles to Round Lake Road. Follow the access signs north for another 1.3 miles to the county landing. A gravel approach to a shallow sand ramp and parking are provided.

RELATED SERVICES
Boat Rentals - Yes.
Resorts - Yes.
Campgrounds - None.

SPECIAL FEATURES - While this lake is somewhat remote, it is well-known and receives considerable fishing pressure.

LAKE CHARACTERISTICS
Size and Depth - 116 acres and 25 feet.
Water Source - Drainage lake: A navigable inlet (Rice Creek) on the east side and a navigable outlet (Rice Creek) on the southwest side.
Shoreline - 10% county-owned.
Bottom - Mostly sand and muck with some gravel.
Water - Extremely fertile and quite clear.
Vegetation - Milfoil, cabbage and coontail are the primary submergent species. There is a well-defined and extensive weedline around the perimeter of the lake.

FISHERY
SPECIES
Primary - Muskie, Bluegill, Perch, Sucker.
Secondary - Largemouth Bass, Walleye, Pumpkinseed, Crappie.
Limited - Northern Pike.
COMMENT - Fluctuations in the northern pike population have occurred. Walleye numbers are sustained by natural reproduction.
FORAGE - Sucker and golden shiner are the primary forage.

LAKE MANAGEMENT
Lake Investigation Data - None recently.
Stocking

ROUND LAKE STOCKING SUMMARY			
YEAR	SPECIES	NUMBER	SIZE
1985	Muskie	200	9"
1987	Muskie	200	8"
1989	Muskie	200	Fingerling

FISHING TIPS - The abundant weed cover, particularly submergent types, is the dominant factor in fishing Round Lake. Work the outside weed edge around the entire lake for muskie, walleye and the occasional northern. Weed points, inside turns, and openings in the weeds are prime locations that produce fish.

An excellent cabbage bed is found on the north shoreline across from the landing. This weedbed extends out from the shoreline point. A hard-bottomed bar extends off the tip of the weed point towards the middle of the lake. Cast this entire area, concentrating on the edges, for muskie and walleye.

The area by the Rice Creek outlet is good for all species of fish. The outlet mouth produces best early in the year. Work the middle of the outlet channel for muskie and northern pike.

Much of the south shoreline has a firm sand/gravel bottom which provides good walleye habitat.

Spring largemouth bass, crappie and other panfish are taken near the edge of the emergent shoreline reeds. Look for something different along shore such as logs, weed openings, or weed points to concentrate fish.

CONCLUSION - The excellent fertility provides a solid foundation for forage and prey species alike. Round Lake holds a surprisingly large number of fish for its small size. However, this out of the way lake is well-known and can receive considerable fishing pressure.

BEAR LAKE

LOCATION - In the northwest part of the book area, west of Highway M and north of Highway K and Little Crooked Lake.

ACCESS - None public.

LAKE CHARACTERISTICS
> **Size and Depth** - 76 acres and 30 feet.
> **Water Source** - Spring-fed lake: An outlet on the northwest end to Round Lake.
> **Shoreline** - 100% privately owned.
> **Bottom** - Primarily sand with some gravel and rock.
> **Water** - Extremely fertile and very clear.
> **Vegetation** - Emergent and submergent varieties are fairly abundant, especially on the northeast end.

FISHERY
> **SPECIES**
>> **Primary** - Walleye, Muskie, Perch, Rock Bass, Sucker.
>> **Secondary** - Smallmouth Bass, Bluegill, Crappie, Bullhead.
>> **Limited** - Largemouth Bass, (Northern Pike).
> **COMMENT** - Walleye are clearly the most abundant gamefish and they show good natural reproduction. Perch are the most common panfish species.

LAKE MANAGEMENT

Lake Investigation Data - None.

Stocking - Limited private stocking occurs. In 1988, 500 walleye fingerling were planted.

FISHING TIPS - The abundant weeds at the northeast end provide good muskie and walleye opportunities. Fish the deep water at the narrows for walleye and at the end of the bay for muskie. Try the outlet end for muskie and the north shore east of the outlet for walleye. Walleye are also found on the point on the north shore. Work for walleye out from the old dock on the east end of the lake.

CONCLUSION - The fishery is well-balanced and in excellent condition. Bear is among the most fertile lakes in the north. Lack of public access restricts fishing.

RICE LAKE

LOCATION - In the northwest corner of the book area, north of Highway K and west of Round Lake Road.

ACCESS - Type IV: On the southwest end of the lake; take Keego Road north from Highway K (just east of Big Lake) north for about ½ mile to an old the logging trail (Keego Road East) and proceed east. The trail is very difficult to negotiate, with much of the area being lowland.

LAKE CHARACTERISTICS

Size and Depth - 9 acres and 15 feet.
Water Source - Seepage lake: No inlet or outlet.
Shoreline -75% state-owned.
Bottom - Primarily muck, with a small area of sand.
Water - Very infertile and brown in color.
Vegetation - Emergent, submergent and floating types are common.

FISHERY

SPECIES - Panfish, (Largemouth Bass).

LAKE MANAGEMENT

Lake Investigation Data - None due to the size of the lake and the inadequate access.
Stocking - None.

CONCLUSION - This extremely small, northwoods "pothole" is so limited in fertility that fishing time is better spent elsewhere.

WOLF LAKE

LOCATION - In the north central part of the section, north of Highway K and Big Crooked Lake and west of Highway M.

ACCESS - None public.

LAKE CHARACTERISTICS
Size and Depth - 393 acres and 28 feet.
Water Source - Drainage lake: An inlet (Wildcat Creek) on the north end from Big Kitten Lake, and an outlet (Wolf Creek) on the southwest end to Little Crooked Lake.
Shoreline - 100% privately owned.
Bottom - Mostly sand and gravel with some rock and muck. The muck is located mainly along the southwest end.
Water - Very fertile and murky.
Vegetation - Abundant weed cover is found mostly along shorelines, midlake bars and in the southwest bay. Both emergent and submergent types are present.

FISHERY
SPECIES
Primary - Muskie, Walleye, Perch, Rock Bass.
Secondary - Smallmouth Bass, Crappie, Bullhead, Bluegill, Pumpkinseed.
Limited - Largemouth Bass.
COMMENT - Walleye are well-established with good year classes and excellent natural reproduction.

LAKE MANAGEMENT
Lake Investigation Data - None.
Stocking - None recently.
Treatment - Fish cribs have been installed.

FISHING TIPS - Walleye and muskie fishing usually begins on the center bars. The large weedy bar near the east shoreline is especially productive. The smaller bar north of this location is also a good walleye spot. The rock bar at the mouth of the southwest bay can offer excellent walleye fishing.

The weed cover of the southwest bay is known for holding muskie. Bucktails worked along the weed edges are usually effective. A weedbed on the northeast side is also a good area for muskie. Both walleye and muskie are usually available from a large weedbed in the southeast bay.

Walleye and smallmouth bass use the old cribs that are found near the lodge.

CONCLUSION - Wolf Lake is a productive and well-balanced fishery. The combination of weeds and hard-bottomed bars with adjacent drop-offs enhances the fishery, but private ownership limits usage.

MAPLE LAKE

LOCATION - In the northwest part of the area, just north of Highway K and east of Big Lake.

ACCESS - Type IV: On the southeast side of the lake; take Maple Lake Road north of Highway K for 0.3 mile to an open field on the left. This is just before a private drive. There is a 300-foot carry-in through the state-owned field to a moderately difficult wilderness landing. Parking is possible along the road.

LAKE CHARACTERISTICS
Size and Depth - 47 acres and 14 feet.
Water Source - Seepage lake: No inlet or outlet.
Shoreline - 75% state-owned.
Bottom - Primarily muck.
Water - Very infertile and quite clear.
Vegetation - Emergent and submergent varieties are present along the shorelines.

FISHERY
SPECIES - Largemouth Bass, Perch, Bluegill, Rock Bass, Pumpkinseed, (Crappie).
COMMENT - Largemouth bass are the only predator species available to hold panfish in check.

LAKE MANAGEMENT
Lake Investigation Data - None.
Stocking - None recently.

CONCLUSION - This fishery is limited by a lack of fertility. Expect slow-growing panfish of small to average size. Largemouth bass numbers are also affected by the infertility. However, a few good-sized bass are reported every year.

LITTLE CROOKED LAKE

LOCATION - In the northwest part of the area, north of Highway K and west of Highway M and Big Crooked Lake.

ACCESS - Type I (Public): On the northwest end of the lake; take Bear Lake Road north off Highway K for 3.3 miles (past Little Crooked and Birch Point

LITTLE CROOKED LAKE

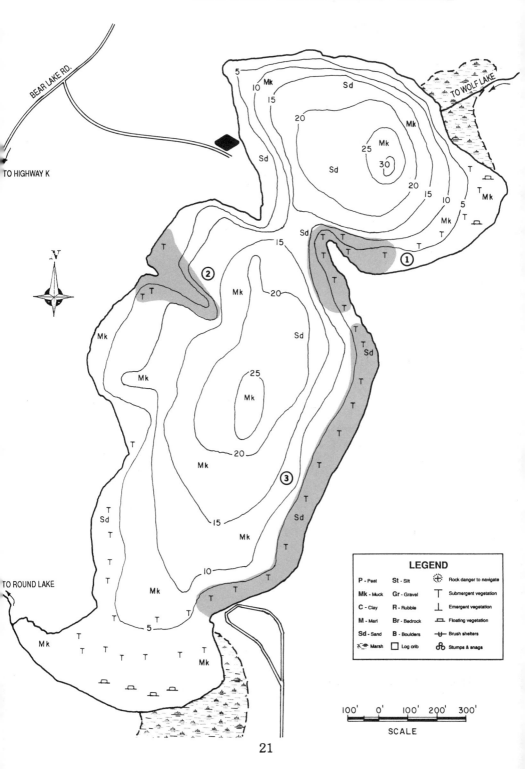

BEAR LAKE RD.

TO HIGHWAY K

TO WOLF LAKE

TO ROUND LAKE

N

① ② ③

LEGEND

P - Peat	St - Silt	⊕ Rock danger to navigate
Mk - Muck	Gr - Gravel	T Submergent vegetation
C - Clay	R - Rubble	⊥ Emergent vegetation
M - Marl	Br - Bedrock	⊡ Floating vegetation
Sd - Sand	B - Boulders	⊔ Brush shelters
☙ Marsh	☐ Log crib	⅋ Stumps & snags

100'   0'   100' 200' 300'

SCALE

21

Roads) to a marked access road. Turn right for a short distance to this state facility. A paved parking area and concrete slab ramp are provided.

RELATED SERVICES
Boat Rentals - Yes.
Resorts - Yes.
Campgrounds - None.

LAKE CHARACTERISTICS
Size and Depth - 153 acres and 25 feet.
Water Source - Drainage lake: An inlet on the north end from Wolf Lake and an outlet on the south end to Rice Creek and Round Lake. Both are considered navigable, but the inlet is quite narrow.
Shoreline - 43% state-owned.
Bottom - 50% muck, 30% sand, 20% gravel.
Water - Very fertile and murky.
Vegetation - Heavy growths of submergent, emergent and floating varieties are present.

FISHERY
SPECIES
Primary - Muskie, Perch, Crappie, Bullhead.
Secondary - Largemouth Bass, Walleye, Bluegill, Pumpkinseed, Rock Bass.
Limited - Smallmouth Bass, (Northern Pike).

COMMENT - Walleye are supplemented by periodic state stocking, though limited natural reproduction is occurring. An abundant population of small bullhead is present. Crappie abundance fluctuates dramatically. Largemouth bass are self-sustaining. Muskie are the dominant predator species and northern pike are scarce.

LAKE MANAGEMENT
Lake Investigation Data - None recently.
Stocking

LITTLE CROOKED LAKE STOCKING SUMMARY			
YEAR	SPECIES	NUMBER	SIZE
1984	Muskie	200	8"
1985	Muskie	225	Fingerling
1986	Walleye	1,400	Fingerling
1988	Walleye	1,450	Fingerling
	Muskie	300	Fingerling
1990	Walleye	300	Fingerling

LAKE SURVEY MAP - Fishing Areas Shaded
Area (1) Work the deep weed edge along this shoreline point for summer muskie.

Bright bucktail spinners are preferred because of the dark water.

Area (2) Backtroll live bait rigs along the edge of this long underwater bar for walleye. Cast in-line spinners and jerkbaits for muskie.

Area (3) This long weedline along the east shore yields largemouth bass, muskie and panfish. Concentrate on inside turns and openings in the weeds for the best bass and panfish action. The best muskie fishing is usually along the deep weed edge.

FISHING TIPS - The abundant weedbeds are the key to success on Little Crooked Lake. Find the weed edges, concentrating on the points, subtle channel openings and inside turns. Look for walleye on the west side along the steeper drop-offs. Because of the dark water color, brightly colored lures are often more effective. Try fishing after dark with surface lures, such as Hawg-Wobblers or Creepers for mid-summer muskie.

CONCLUSION - This lake has a decent and varied fishery for its size. Try working it for a legal muskie.

BIG CROOKED LAKE (CLEAR CROOKED LAKE)

LOCATION - In the north central part of the section, north of Highway K and west of Highway M.

ACCESS - Type V: A narrow, shallow outlet creek is located on the south end from Boulder Lake.

LAKE CHARACTERISTICS
> **Size and Depth** - 682 acres and 38 feet.
> **Water Source** - Drained lake: An outlet with moderate flow on the south end to Boulder Lake.
> **Shoreline** - 100% privately owned. The two islands on the south end are state-owned.
> **Bottom** - Sand and gravel.
> **Water** - Moderately infertile and fairly clear.
> **Vegetation** - Limited to the shoreline zones except for the south bay. Both emergent and submergent varieties are present.

FISHERY
> **SPECIES**
>> **Primary** - Walleye, Perch, Rock Bass, Sucker.
>> **Secondary** - Muskie, Smallmouth Bass, Bluegill, Pumpkinseed.
>> **Limited** - Largemouth Bass, Crappie, (Northern Pike).

COMMENT - Walleye are the most popular species and natural reproduction is occurring.

LAKE MANAGEMENT
    Lake Investigation Data - None recently.
    Stocking - None recently.
    Treatment - Cribs have been installed.

FISHING TIPS - Both walleye and decent-size perch relate to the large sand/gravel point that extends out from the golf course. The bar on the west side drops off into deep water and often produces walleye.

On the west side of the lake, south of the lodge, old cribs provide cover for smallmouth, walleye and perch. The cribs extend to the rubble point. In summer and fall, work the drop-offs for muskie.

A rock bar extends in an east-west direction from the island. Cast this structure for walleye, smallmouth and muskie. Another deep bar is found northeast of the island that attracts walleye during midsummer. A depthfinder is needed to effectively work this structure.

Muskie, walleye and perch are present in the submerged weeds found in the southern bay.

CONCLUSION - Big Crooked Lake offers good fishing for walleye, smallmouth bass, muskie and perch. However, lack of public access limits fishing to relatively few anglers.

WHITNEY LAKE (HARRINGTON LAKE)

LOCATION - In the northwest part of the area, south of Highway K and west of Highway H.

ACCESS - Type III: On the east side of the lake; take Whitney Lake Road southwest off Highway K for 1.0 mile, then stay to the right for 0.1 mile to the end of the road. This municipal landing has an easy 150-foot carry-in to the beach of a shallow bay.

SPECIAL FEATURES - Only electric motors are permitted.

LAKE CHARACTERISTICS
    Size and Depth - 102 acres and 8 feet.
    Water Source - Spring-fed lake: An outlet on the southwest end through a creek to the Manitowish River.
    Shoreline - 50% state-owned land. 90% bog-lined.
    Bottom - Muck with some sand.
    Water - Moderately fertile and fairly clear. Winterkill occurs periodically.
    Vegetation - Extensive areas of submergent, emergent and floating varieties are present in most of the lake.

FISHERY
SPECIES
Primary - Northern Pike, Perch.
Secondary - Largemouth Bass, Sunfish, Bullhead.
Limited - Crappie, (Muskie).
COMMENT - The occasional winterkill limits the fishery potential. However, only minor fish kills have been reported. Northern pike and perch usually survive low oxygen levels. Winter oxygen levels are marginal in the top layer, and usually intolerable for fish a few feet below the surface.

Perch and sunfish are present in good numbers. Northern pike and largemouth bass are the primary predators. There is speculation that a few muskie may also be present.

LAKE MANAGEMENT
Lake Investigation Data - None recently.
Stocking - None recently.

FISHING TIPS - Expect logs, stumps and weed edges to provide the best action. Successful bass and northern pike anglers usually work the weedline with spinnerbaits and small crankbaits.

CONCLUSION - Recently, fishing has become more popular on Whitney Lake with an emphasis on perch and northern pike. At times, success has been good.

WOOL LAKE

LOCATION - In the northwest part of the area, north of the Highway K/H intersection.

ACCESS - Type IV: On the southwest end of the lake; from the Highway K/H intersection, proceed north on Highway K for 1.0 mile. A difficult ¼-mile carry-in is possible from Highway K. Proceed in a northeast direction through the woods to insure staying on state land.

LAKE CHARACTERISTICS
Size and Depth - 33 acres and 45 feet.
Water Source - Seepage lake: No inlet or outlet.
Shoreline - 17% state-owned, entirely at the southwest end.
Bottom - 70% sand, 20% gravel, 10% rock.
Water - Fairly infertile and quite clear. Oxygen levels are good down to 35 feet.
Vegetation - Very limited; confined to a narrow shoreline fringe.

FISHERY

SPECIES
Primary - Smallmouth Bass, Rock Bass, Perch.
Secondary - Pumpkinseed, Crappie, Sucker.
Limited - Walleye, (Largemouth Bass).
COMMENT - Smallmouth bass, though small in size, are the dominant gamefish. A limited number of walleye are present.

Rock bass dominate the panfish, with pumpkinseed and crappie present in lesser numbers. However, sizes of all panfish are small.

LAKE MANAGEMENT
Lake Investigation Data - None recently.
Stocking - None recently.

FISHING TIPS - Fishing is difficult as the lack of structure and vegetation means that fish can be found anywhere. The remnants of some old fish cribs still might hold a few fish. Four are located in the northeast bay, three along the north shore point, and three along the south shore from the point to the southeast bay.

CONCLUSION - The lack of adequate public access limits fishing pressure on Wool Lake. Don't expect trophies, but small bass and panfish action.

BOULDER LAKE

LOCATION - In the north central part of the area, immediately northwest of Boulder Junction.

ACCESS

A **Type I (Public):** At the west end of the lake on the Manitowish River outlet; from just west of the Highway H/K intersection, turn north on Lucas Lane for several hundred feet. There is an unimproved sand/gravel ramp and limited parking.

B **Type I (Public):** On the north side of the lake at the private airport; take Airport Road west from Highway M for 1.4 miles to the landing. A concrete ramp and parking are provided.

Type V: To the east end of the lake, via the Manitowish River. There is a steep but short Type III access at Highway M. Parking is limited along the road.

RELATED SERVICES
Boat Rentals - Yes.
Resorts - Yes.
Campgrounds - None.

LAKE CHARACTERISTICS

Size and Depth - 524 acres and 23 feet.

Water Source - Drainage lake: An inlet on the east end from the Manitowish River and a minor inlet on the northwest end from Big Crooked Lake. An outlet on the west end to the Manitowish River.

Shoreline - 23% state-owned; on the southwest end. The island on the east end is also state-owned.

Bottom - 50% sand, 30% gravel, 10% muck, 10% rock.

Water - Moderately fertile and slightly murky.

Vegetation - Very limited, mainly along the shoreline.

FISHERY

SPECIES

Primary - Muskie, Walleye, Perch.

Secondary - Largemouth Bass, Smallmouth Bass, Crappie, Bluegill, Pumpkinseed, Bullhead.

Limited - Northern Pike.

COMMENT - Walleye abundance and size ranges are very good. Natural reproduction is considered above average. Also, Boulder Lake is rated as Class A muskie water.

FORAGE - Crayfish are abundant, including rusty crayfish. Perch and various minnow species also contribute to the forage base.

LAKE MANAGEMENT

Lake Investigation Data - A recent spring fyke netting survey was conducted by the Wisconsin Department of Natural Resources to estimate the walleye population.

Based on the survey results, the adult walleye population was estimated at approximately 1,625 fish with a density of 3.1 fish per acre.

BOULDER LAKE FYKE NET SUMMARY		
SPECIES	SIZE RANGE	NUMBER
Walleye	7" - 11.9"	109
Walleye	12" - 14.9"	521
Walleye	15" - 19.9"	399
Walleye	20" - 28.4"	47

Stocking

BOULDER LAKE STOCKING SUMMARY			
YEAR	SPECIES	NUMBER	SIZE
1981	Muskie	400	12"
1983	Muskie	1,000	11"
1984	Largemouth Bass	1,000	Fingerling
	Bluegill	500	--
1985	Muskie	1,000	Fingerling
1989	Muskie	500	11"

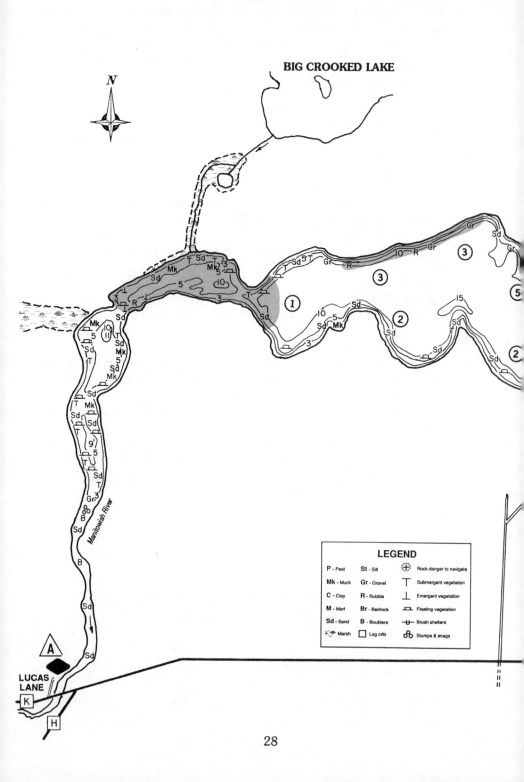

BIG CROOKED LAKE

N

LEGEND

P - Peat	St - Silt	Rock danger to navigate
Mk - Muck	Gr - Gravel	Submergent vegetation
C - Clay	R - Rubble	Emergent vegetation
M - Marl	Br - Bedrock	Floating vegetation
Sd - Sand	B - Boulders	Brush shelters
Marsh	Log crib	Stumps & snags

Manitowish River

LUCAS
LANE

A

K

H

28

BOULDER LAKE

TO HIGHWAY M

AIRPORT ROAD

Manitowish River

BOULDER JUNCTION

500'   0'   500'   1000'   1500'

SCALE

LAKE SURVEY MAP - Fishing Areas Shaded

Area (1) Weeds dominate the west outlet end to the Manitowish River. Largemouth bass, muskie and panfish relate to the deep submergent weed edges. Fish this area early in the season before weed growth becomes heavy.

Area (2) Check the three bays on the south shore for largemouth. Concentrate on the weedline that usually consists of floating weeds. Both points on the south side have sand bottoms that attract walleye.

Area (3) The north shoreline offers a rapid drop-off from 3 to 10 feet. Work jig/minnow combos along the gravel, sand and rock bottom for walleye and an occasional smallmouth bass. This entire area produces best early in the season.

Area (4) Fish the underwater gravel bar, concentrating on the 10-foot depths for walleye. If action is slow, work toward the 20-foot hole.

Area (5) This long gravel point on the north side is a popular walleye area.

Area (6) Work the edge of the reef for muskie and smallmouth. During windy conditions, fish move onto the shallow rocks to feed. The 10- to 20-foot depths hold summer walleye. The shallow rocks can pose a navigation hazard.

Area (7) The north side of this small island has a rock bar that drops off into deep water. Walleye, smallmouth and even an occasional muskie relate to this structure. Use your depthfinder to stay on the 8- to 20-foot break.

Area (8) Warming inlet currents of the Manitowish River are a positive early spring influence. Deeper weed edges (both submergent and emergent) can yield muskie, bass, walleye and panfish.

Area (9) Several old cribs are found approximately 1,500 feet northwest of the inlet (about 300 feet off shore). Even in deteriorated condition, they can produce panfish, bass or walleye.

Area (10) A gentle sloping bar off the east shoreline (near the airport) can produce both walleye and muskie. The 10-foot edge of the bar and some old cribs tend to hold most of the fish.

FISHING TIPS - Boulder Lake can challenge anglers since both weedbeds and structure are limited. However, the murky water means that fish tend to remain shallow due to limited light penetration.

Dark water warrants the use of brightly colored lures. Subtle structure breaks in combination with gravel/sand bottom components are important to finding fish.

CONCLUSION - Despite moderate to heavy fishing pressure, Boulder Lake produces good numbers of walleye and muskie. The lake is capable of yielding a trophy muskie in the 20- to 25-pound category. It has a local reputation, however, of providing sharply varying fishing success from year to year.

LITTLE RICE LAKE

LOCATION - In the north central part of the area, just east of Boulder Junction.

ACCESS

Type III: On the west end of the lake; from Highway M, take Little Rice Road east for 0.3 mile to this municipal facility. Little Rice Road is just north of the triangle intersection at the east end of town. A gravel road leads to a small gravel parking area near the heavily weeded shore.

Type V: On the northeast side of the lake; navigable access is possible through the Manitowish River. A small boat or canoe can be launched downstream at the Highway M bridge.

SPECIAL FEATURES - Electric motors only.

LAKE CHARACTERISTICS
Size and Depth - 59 acres and 7 feet.
Water Source - Spring-fed lake: An outlet to the Manitowish River on the northeast end.
Shoreline - 20% state-owned, entirely on the south side.
Bottom - Mostly muck.
Water - Moderately fertile and murky.
Vegetation - Heavy throughout the lake, especially emergent and floating.

FISHERY
SPECIES - Muskie, Northern Pike, Walleye, Largemouth Bass, Crappie, Perch, Pumpkinseed, Rock Bass, Bluegill, Sucker.
COMMENT - Little Rice Lake can be thought of as part of the Manitowish River. Species move between the lake and river. Good numbers of northern, walleye and even muskie are present. The DNR has rated this lake Class C for muskie. Crappie and perch are the primary panfish species.

LAKE MANAGEMENT
Lake Investigation Data - None recently.
Stocking - None recently.

FISHING TIPS - The weeds so totally dominate this lake that fishing efforts should be confined to early spring. Obviously, fishing this lake means working weed edges and open holes. At times, it has provided surprisingly good muskie fishing.

CONCLUSION - Little Rice Lake contains fairly balanced numbers of gamefish and panfish. Due to difficult access, fishing pressure remains light.

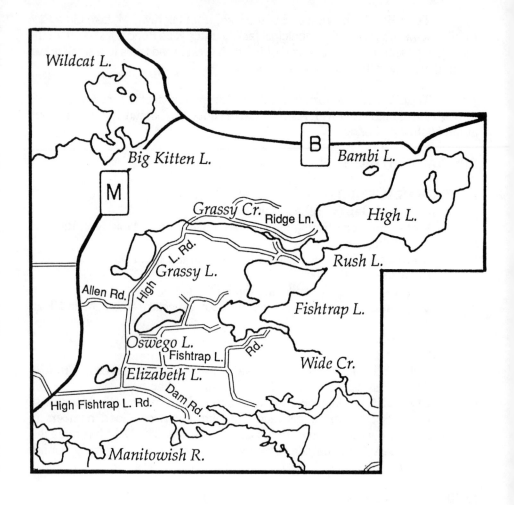

Wildcat Lake   **Rush Lake**
Big Kitten Lake   **High Lake**
Grassy Lake   **Bambi Lake**
Oswego Lake   **Elizabeth Lake**
Fishtrap Lake   **Manitowish River**

WILDCAT LAKE

LOCATION - In the north central part of the area, immediately west of Highway M and south of Highway B.

ACCESS - Type I (Public): On the southeast end of the lake; this marked landing is adjacent to Highway M. There is a paved parking area, turn-around, concrete slab ramp and loading pier.

RELATED SERVICES
Boat Rentals - Yes.
Resorts - Yes.
Campgrounds - Yes, one state wilderness site.

LAKE CHARACTERISTICS
Size and Depth - 316 acres and 35 feet.
Water Source - Drainage lake: Pond Creek inlets on the north side and a navigable outlet on the southwest end to Big Kitten Lake.
Shoreline - 17% state-owned land, entirely on the south end.
Bottom - 55% sand, 30% muck, 10% gravel, 5% rock.
Water - Exceptionally fertile and a little murky.
Vegetation - Heavy weed growth along the shoreline consists of cabbage, coontail, reeds, and lily pads. The west side has broad flats of submergent weeds.

FISHERY
SPECIES
Primary - Muskie, Walleye, Crappie, Bluegill.
Secondary - Largemouth Bass, Perch, Rock Bass, Bullhead.
Limited - Smallmouth Bass, Pumpkinseed.
COMMENT - Muskie and walleye numbers are maintained by state stocking. Yearly fluctuations in the walleye population have occurred. Crappie are generally abundant throughout the lake and obtain decent size.

LAKE MANAGEMENT
Lake Investigation Data - A recent electrofishing study observed that poor walleye reproduction was occurring. Only 17 young-of-the-year fish were seen.

WILDCAT LAKE ELECTROFISHING SUMMARY		
SPECIES	NUMBER	MAX. SIZE
Walleye	29	24"
Muskie	16	30"
Largemouth Bass	5	15.5"
Smallmouth Bass	9	13"

The study confirmed that walleye are being sustained by state plantings.

Stocking

WILDCAT LAKE STOCKING SUMMARY			
YEAR	**SPECIES**	**NUMBER**	**SIZE**
1983	Muskie	600	9"
1985	Muskie	600	9"
1986	Walleye	4,400	3"
1987	Muskie	1,000	8"
	Walleye	15,000	Fingerling
1989	Walleye	20,985	Fingerling

LAKE SURVEY MAP - Fishing Areas Shaded

Area (1) The bay by the boat landing has emergent and submergent weeds together with small areas of gravel that attract many species of fish. A small underwater point just outside the weedline is used by walleye. The small cove on the north side provides a mixture of cover that holds crappie and largemouth bass. Work the deep weed edge along the southern portion of the bay for muskie, bass and crappie. Early in the season, muskie can be found in the shallows. During summer and fall, the 5- to 10-foot depths generally produce the best action.

Area (2) The scattered vegetation on this gravel and rock bottom attracts muskie, walleye and an occasional smallmouth. During summer, muskie anglers should target the 5- to 15-foot depths.

Area (3) This northern bay often holds largemouth and muskie on the deep weed edge.

Area (4) Work the weedbeds found around this northern point and the nearby gravel bar for muskie and an occasional walleye.

Area (5) This large weedbed offers prime habitat for panfish, largemouth bass, muskie and walleye. The deeper weeds, between 5 and 11 feet, provide consistent action. During summer, work the slop found along the shoreline for largemouth.

Area (6) Cast deep-diving crankbaits along the steep drop-off on the north side of this westernmost island for walleye. The scattered weeds on the northeast side yield both walleye and muskie.

Area (7) The south side of the large island has a steep drop-off and a hard bottom. Backtroll live bait rigs along this structure for walleye.

Area (8) The north side of the large island has scattered logs and weeds and should be worked for largemouth, muskie and crappie.

Area (9) Fish the rock bottom off the north, south and east sides of this island for walleye.

Area (10) The weedy drop-offs around these islands produce walleye in spring and after dark. Pay close attention to the north and east sides of the islands.

FISHING TIPS - Wildcat Lake offers a wide variety of structure. Abundant vegetation allows weedline fishing for all species. Natural colored bucktails work well for muskie.

34

WILDCAT LAKE

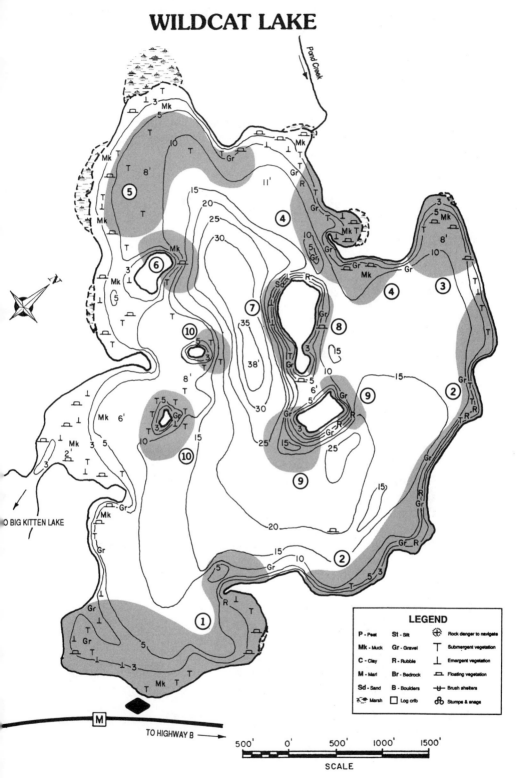

LEGEND

P - Peat	**St** - Silt	⊕ Rock danger to navigate
Mk - Muck	**Gr** - Gravel	⊤ Submergent vegetation
C - Clay	**R** - Rubble	⊥ Emergent vegetation
M - Marl	**Br** - Bedrock	⊏⊐ Floating vegetation
Sd - Sand	**B** - Boulders	⊔ Brush shelters
	≋ Marsh	☐ Log crib	♣ Stumps & snags

Pond Creek

TO BIG KITTEN LAKE

TO HIGHWAY B →

M

SCALE

500'   0'   500'   1000'   1500'

Walleye anglers use jig and minnows early, switching to leeches by early June, and back to minnows in September. Slip bobber rigging is effective along the weedline.

Bass are underfished and offer trophy potential. Spinnerbaits, balsa minnows and crankbaits produce. Crappie fishing varies from year to year but is generally very good.

CONCLUSION - Wildcat Lake is a productive fishery for both gamefish and panfish, particularly when taking into consideration the heavy pressure it receives. Muskie fishing, especially for a first legal, is popular.

BIG KITTEN LAKE

LOCATION - In the north central part of the area, immediately west of Highway M and south of Highway B. It is about 3½ miles north of Boulder Junction.

ACCESS - Type V: Navigable access is possible from Wildcat Lake through the channel at the northeast end of the lake.

RELATED SERVICES
> **Boat Rentals** - Yes, at the resort.
> **Resorts** - Yes.
> **Campgrounds** - None.

LAKE CHARACTERISTICS
> **Size and Depth** - 51 acres and 22 feet.
> **Water Source** - Drainage lake: An inlet on the north end from Wildcat Lake and an outlet on the west side (Wildcat Creek) to Wolf Lake.
> **Shoreline** - 50% state-owned land, primarily on the northeast and west sides.
> **Bottom** - Mostly sand, with gravel and some rock and muck.
> **Water** - Exceptionally fertile and a little murky.
> **Vegetation** - Emergent, submergent and floating varieties are abundant on the shorelines and in the bays.

FISHERY
> **SPECIES**
>> **Primary** - Muskie, Crappie, Perch, Rock Bass, Bullhead.
>> **Secondary** - Largemouth Bass, Bluegill, Pumpkinseed.
>> **Limited** - Walleye, Smallmouth Bass.
>
> **COMMENT** - The state rates the lake as Class A muskie water, but the walleye population appears to be low. Panfish are an important part of the fishery.

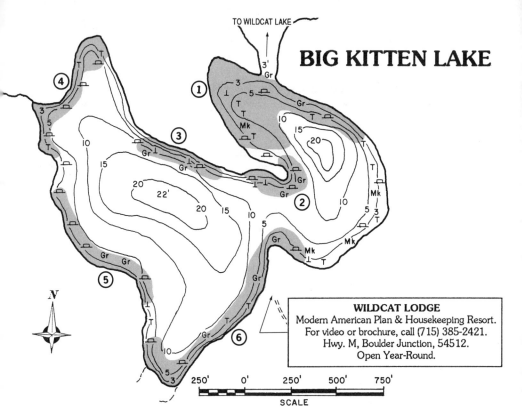

BIG KITTEN LAKE

WILDCAT LODGE
Modern American Plan & Housekeeping Resort.
For video or brochure, call (715) 385-2421.
Hwy. M, Boulder Junction, 54512.
Open Year-Round.

LAKE MANAGEMENT
Lake Investigation Data - None.
Stocking - None recently.

LAKE SURVEY MAP - Fishing Areas Shaded
Area (1) The inlet bay (from Wildcat Lake) has heavy growths of lily pads, reeds and cabbage. Both gamefish and panfish relate to these weed edges.
The northeast shoreline has a gravel bottom that holds smallmouth and large-mouth bass. Crappie and muskie are found west of the inlet mouth along the deep weed edge. Use presentations that effectively work the weed edges. In early spring, largemouth use the shallow weed cover.
Area (2) This shoreline point has a gravel bottom and scattered weed growth that attract walleye, muskie and largemouth.
Area (3) The firm gravel bottom and abundant weeds hold walleye and smallmouth. Most action is found along the drop-off.
Area (4) The northwest bay, adjacent to Wildcat Creek outlet, offers perch, crappie and largemouth bass. Weeds of all types dominate the shoreline. Cast the deep weedline, keying on inside turns and weed pockets.
Area (5) Floating weeds, especially lily pads, are found along this gravel shoreline. Muskie, smallmouth bass and even an occasional walleye are taken from the available cover.

Area (6) The southeast shore, including the prominent point, contain both emergent and submergent weeds. Work south and west of the point for muskie and largemouth.

FISHING TIPS - Weed cover and steep shoreline breaks attract the majority of angling attention. There really are no secrets here, as the shoreline weed edges offer most of the fishing action.

CONCLUSION - This lake can offer an interesting side trip from the moderate to heavy fishing pressure on Wildcat Lake. Remember that Big Kitten Lake does not have much in the way of submerged structure.

GRASSY LAKE (JEAN LAKE)

LOCATION - In the north central part of the area, just east of Highway M, about 2½ miles north of Boulder Junction.

ACCESS

Type III: On the east side of the lake; take Allen Road east off Highway M to High Lake Road and turn left to the access. The landing is adjacent to High Lake Road at the lake sign. There is a fairly short carry-in to a shallow, weedy landing. Roadside parking is available.

Type III: On the northeast side of the lake; take High Lake Road 0.3 mile north of the first landing. There is a similar carry-in to the lake, but there is an off-road parking area.

LAKE CHARACTERISTICS
Size and Depth - 38 acres and 8 feet.
Water Source - Spring-fed lake: An outlet on the north end to Grassy Creek and Rush Lake.
Shoreline - 80% state-owned land; the entire east portion of the lake.
Bottom - Muck and some sand.
Water - Quite fertile and very murky. Winterkill is normally an annual problem.
Vegetation - Abundant weeds choke the lake. Most common varieties are present.

FISHERY
SPECIES - Northern Pike, Perch, Bullhead, (Largemouth Bass), (Muskie).
COMMENT - Expect a limited perch fishery as winterkill is the controlling factor. It is doubtful that bass or muskie contribute much to the fishery.

LAKE MANAGEMENT
Lake Investigation Data - None recently.
Stocking - None recently.

CONCLUSION - While this lake is good for canoe outings, there is nothing here to attract fishing interest.

OSWEGO LAKE

LOCATION - In the north central part of the area, east of Highway M and about 2 miles north of Boulder Junction.

ACCESS - Type III: On the east end of the lake; from Highway M, take High-Fishtrap Lake Road east to Fishtrap Road. Follow Oswego-Fishtrap Lake Road to the landing. There is limited parking along the road and a short carry-in to a sand beach.

RELATED SERVICES
Boat Rentals - Yes, at the resort.
Resorts - Yes.
Campgrounds - None.

SPECIAL FEATURES - Electric motors only.

LAKE CHARACTERISTICS
Size and Depth - 66 acres and 17 feet.
Water Source - Seepage lake: No inlet or outlet.
Shoreline - 50% state-owned, on the north and east sides.
Bottom - 75% sand, 15% gravel, 10% muck.
Water - Very infertile and quite clear. There is a history of periodic and moderate winterkill.
Vegetation - Common in most areas of the lake. Apparently, submergent weeds have declined in recent years.

FISHERY
SPECIES
Primary - Northern Pike, Bluegill, Perch, Bullhead.
Secondary - Largemouth Bass, Pumpkinseed, Rock Bass.
Limited - Walleye, Muskie, (Crappie).
COMMENT - Panfish species are numerous and apparently slow growing. Bluegill are the most abundant panfish followed by perch, pumpkinseed and bullhead. Rock bass are found up to 8 inches, while crappie are very limited. Largemouth bass are present in good numbers, but are small in size. Only small numbers of big northern pike are available which accounts for the abundant panfish.

LAKE MANAGEMENT

Lake Investigation Data - None recently.
Stocking - In 1987, 300 adult northern pike were planted.

FISHING TIPS - Weeds are the key to finding fish. Area residents report that northern pike and muskie have been taken up to 35 inches. Work the weed edges with bucktails and spinnerbaits for both species. Bass appear to be an underfished resource. Remember that even the small gamefish are important in keeping abundant panfish in check.

CONCLUSION - Oswego Lake is fairly difficult to fish due to the absence of shoreline structure and defined weedlines. Panfishing might be a good bet for youngsters or family outings.

FISHTRAP LAKE

LOCATION - In the northeast part of the area, east of Highway M and south of Highway B and High Lake.

ACCESS

A **Type III:** On the north side of the lake just east of the channel to Rush Lake; take High-Fishtrap Lake Road east off Highway M to High Lake Road. Proceed north on High Lake Road to Ridge Road. Drive right and follow this road to the landing on the east side of the culvert. There is a short, but fairly steep, carry-in to the gravel shore. Roadside parking is available.

B **Type III:** On the west side of the lake; take High-Fishtrap Lake Road off Highway M to High Lake Road. Proceed north a short distance to Oswego-Fishtrap Lake Road. Turn right and follow this road to the north. The sand landing is just a few feet from the road through the brush. Roadside parking is limited.

Type V: Navigable access from High and Rush Lakes via the channel on the north side.

RELATED SERVICES

Boat Rentals - Yes, at the resorts.
Resorts - Yes.
Campgrounds - Yes.

LAKE CHARACTERISTICS

Size and Depth - 329 acres and 41 feet.
Water Source - Drainage lake: A navigable inlet on the north side from Rush Lake and a navigable outlet on the southeast end to the Manitowish River. There is a low-head dam at the outlet.

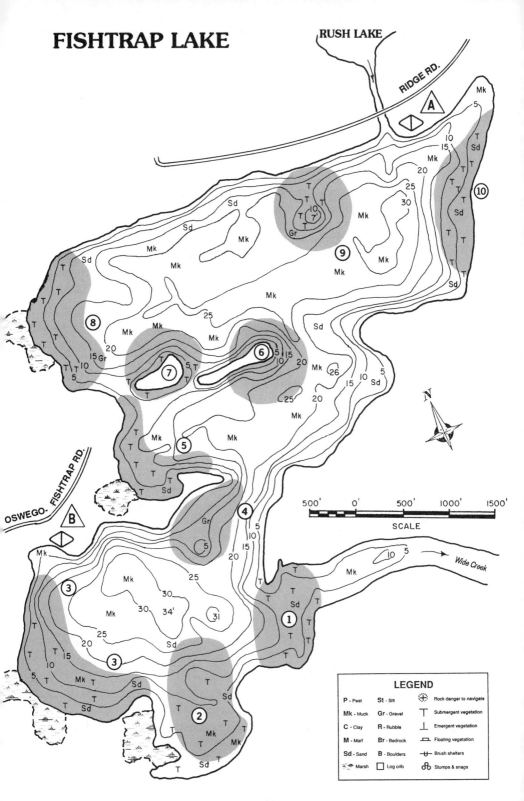

FISHTRAP LAKE

Shoreline - 20% state-owned; the east side and a small section of the west side.

Bottom - 40% sand, 25% gravel, 20% muck, 15% rock.

Water - Exceptionally fertile and fairly clear.

Vegetation - Moderate densities of water lily, milfoil, pickerel weed and wild celery.

FISHERY

SPECIES

Primary - Walleye, Muskie, Perch, Rock Bass.

Secondary - Northern Pike, Largemouth Bass, Crappie, Bluegill, Pumpkinseed.

Limited - Smallmouth Bass, Bullhead, Grass Pickerel.

COMMENT - Walleye and muskie populations are excellent. The state has rated this lake as Class A muskie water. A recent increase in northern pike has negatively impacted muskie numbers. Muskie are largely sustained by state stocking. Crappie numbers can fluctuate dramatically, but strong year classes can produce some outstanding fishing.

LAKE MANAGEMENT

Lake Investigation Data - A recent electrofishing survey to assess walleye reproduction concluded that a strong 1985 year class was the result of natural reproduction. Additionally, good numbers of fish 2 to 4 years old were seen. Year-to-year fluctuations in walleye year class strength have been noted. The following chart is a summary of fish taken in this survey.

FISHTRAP LAKE ELECTROFISHING SUMMARY		
SPECIES	NUMBER	MAX. SIZE
Walleye	210	17"
Muskie	8	20"
Smallmouth Bass	13	11"
Largemouth Bass	13	16"
Grass Pickerel	4	11"

Stocking

FISHTRAP LAKE STOCKING SUMMARY			
YEAR	SPECIES	NUMBER	SIZE
1982	Muskie	600	8"
1984	Muskie	240	8"
1985	Muskie	600	8"
1987	Muskie	600	8"
1989	Muskie	300	11"

LAKE SURVEY MAP - Fishing Areas Shaded

Area (1) The submergent weed edge at the mouth of the outlet stream (to Manitowish River) yields muskie and northern pike. Work the 8- to 12-foot weedline with in-line spinners and jerkbaits. Northern pike in the 4- to 8-pound range have been taken as well as several 12- to 15-pound trophies.

Area (2) The weeds in this bay attract panfish, bass, walleye and muskie. Drift or use your electric motor and cast parallel to the well-defined deep weedline, concentrating on the inside turns, points and channels.

Area (3) Muskie, northern pike and panfish relate to the weed growth on this gradually sloping bottom. Some excellent catches of crappie have been reported. Key on the deep weed edge in the 10- to 13-foot depths.

Area (4) Cast the edges of the gravel hump for walleye and smallmouth. The top of the bar is productive for feeding smallmouth bass, especially early or late in the day.

Area (5) This small bay on the west shoreline produces largemouth bass. Cast parallel to the deep weedline with plastic worms or jig n' pig combos.

Area (6) The island near the center of the lake provides steep drop-offs that attract walleye and smallmouth bass. Work the 10- to 20-foot depths with live bait presentations.

Area (7) Muskie and panfish use the weed growth around this small island.

Area (8) Abundant vegetation and deep weed edges provide muskie, pike and panfish action in the northwest corner of the lake. Walleye are taken on the gravel bottom at the south end of the weedbed near the island.

Area (9) This weedy, 7- to 10-foot bar has a good weedline adjacent to the 20- to 25-foot depths. Work the gravel at the south edge of the bar for walleye and smallmouth. Muskie and panfish are usually found on top of the bar.

Area (10) This shallow weedbed extends well out from shore before dropping to the deepest water of the lake. The shallow weed edges hold panfish and an occasional muskie, while deeper breaks should be fished for walleye.

FISHING TIPS - Weeds are often the most important element to establishing a pattern on Fishtrap Lake. Look for the deep weedlines to attract a majority of the action. Concentrate on inside turns, changes in weed types and weed points. Cast parallel to the weedlines whenever possible. Jigs and minnows are popular for walleye early in the season while leeches take over by June. Slip bobber rigs are effective for working the shallow weed growth. Bucktails, especially in black or fluorescent colors, are good muskie producers.

CONCLUSION - Fishtrap Lake has an excellent fishery that includes good numbers of gamefish and panfish. Clearly, Fishtrap Lake deserves your attention.

RUSH LAKE

LOCATION - In the northeast part of the area, east of Highway M, south of Highway B, and immediately north of Fishtrap Lake.

ACCESS - Type III: To the south end of the lake; take High-Fishtrap Lake Road east off Highway M to High Lake Road. Proceed north on High Lake Road to Ridge Road. Drive right and follow this road to the landing on the east side of the culvert. There is a short, but fairly steep, carry-in to a gravel shore. Go through the culvert under the road into Rush Lake. There is some roadside parking available.

SPECIAL FEATURES - Rush Lake is a shallow bay between High and Fishtrap Lakes.

LAKE CHARACTERISTICS

Size and Depth - 44 acres and 7 feet.

Water Source - Drainage lake: An inlet on the north end from High Lake and an outlet on the south end to Fishtrap Lake.

Shoreline - 10% state-owned, in the northwest corner. Town road right-of-way is near the channel on the south end.

Bottom - Mostly muck with sand and some gravel.

Water - Extremely fertile and a little murky.

Vegetation - Abundant weeds and bog edges. A midlake channel remains open due to boat traffic.

FISHERY

SPECIES - Largemouth Bass, Walleye, Northern Pike, Muskie, Perch, Bluegill, Pumpkinseed, Crappie, Bullhead.

COMMENT - As a shallow bay of High Lake, Rush Lake is capable of holding any of the High Lake species at anytime, especially in spring. Apparently, largemouth bass, panfish, walleye, and an occasional northern pike can be found along the weed edges.

CONCLUSION - Rather than as a fishery, Rush Lake is more important as a connecting thoroughfare to Fishtrap and High Lakes.

HIGH LAKE

LOCATION - In the northeast portion of the book area, just south of Highway B, and about 3 miles east of Highway M.

ACCESS

⚠️A **Type I (Public):** On the north end of the lake, adjacent to Highway B, 3.7 miles east of the Highway M/B intersection. A gravel ramp, loading pier and gravel parking area for 15 rigs are present.

⚠️B **Type III:** On the north end of Fishtrap Lake; take High-Fishtrap Lake Road east off Highway M to High Lake Road. Proceed north on High Lake Road to Ridge Road. Drive right and follow this road to the landing on the east side of the culvert. There is a short, but fairly steep, carry-in to the gravel shore of Fishtrap Lake and limited roadside parking. Go through the culvert, north through the Rush Lake channel, and out into the southwest end of High Lake.

RELATED SERVICES
Boat Rentals - Yes, at resorts.
Resorts - Yes.
Campgrounds - None, but there are 4 picnic and canoe campsites.

LAKE CHARACTERISTICS
Size and Depth - 734 acres and 31 feet.
Water Source - Drainage lake: A small inlet on the north side and an outlet on the southwest end to Rush Lake.
Shoreline - 25% state-owned; on the east side and the northwest side. The islands are also state-owned.
Bottom - 35% sand, 25% gravel, 20% rock, 20% muck.
Water - Exceptionally fertile and fairly clear.
Vegetation - Moderate densities of emergent, submergent and floating varieties. Heavier weed concentrations are seen in the shallows of the north end.

FISHERY
SPECIES
Primary - Muskie, Walleye, Perch, Crappie.
Secondary - Largemouth Bass, Bluegill, Pumpkinseed, Bullhead, Rock Bass.
Limited - Northern Pike, Smallmouth Bass.
COMMENT - Walleye and muskie dominate the gamefish species. Walleye average slightly larger than those in Fishtrap Lake. The state rates High Lake as Class A muskie water. Crappie and perch numbers appear to fluctuate dramatically, though they are often abundant. Largemouth bass are secondary in interest but are stable in numbers with many large fish.

LAKE MANAGEMENT
Lake Investigation Data - None recently.
Stocking

HIGH LAKE STOCKING SUMMARY			
YEAR	SPECIES	NUMBER	SIZE
1982	Muskie	1,400	8"
1984	Muskie	1,050	Fingerling
1985	Muskie	5	9"
1988	Muskie	1,400	Fingerling
1990	Muskie	1,229	Fingerling

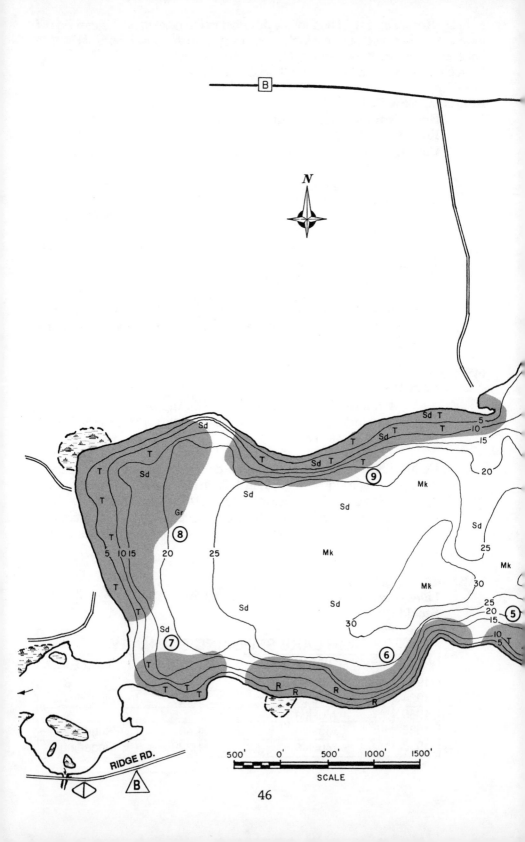

RIDGE RD.

500' 0' 500' 1000' 1500'

SCALE

46

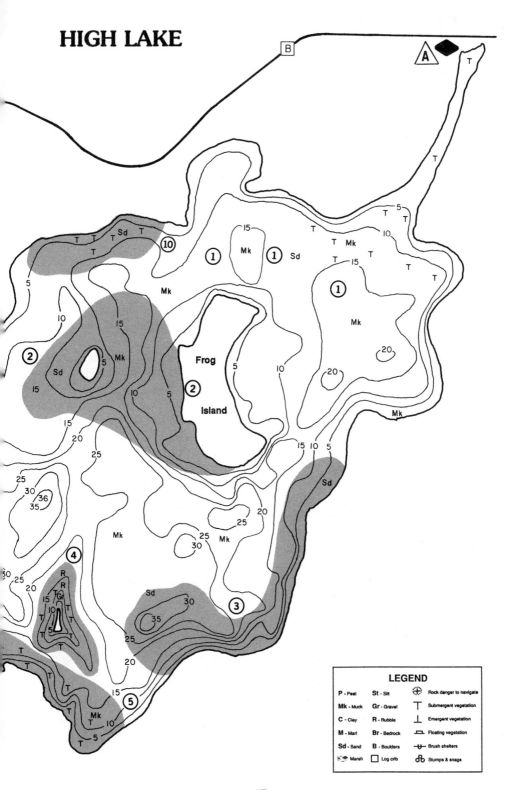

HIGH LAKE

LAKE SURVEY MAP - Fishing Areas Shaded

Area (1) The shallow northeast section of the lake attracts muskie, bass and panfish. Work the submergent vegetation with spinnerbaits for muskie and bass. Early in the season, cast slip bobber combinations over the developing weed cover for crappie and perch.

Area (2) The area between Frog Island and the small island to the west is famous for muskie. Mepps Giant Killers and surface lures can effectively cover the shallow water. Walleye are often found on the deep water break south of the islands.

Area (3) This hard-bottomed area along the east shore attracts walleye and muskie. Use a depthfinder to locate subtle breaks and variations in bottom content. This spot has a local reputation for fall muskie fishing.

Area (4) Weeds and the rock bottom around this island hold walleye and smallmouth bass. Backtroll live bait rigs along the gravel/rubble bottom north of the island for walleye. During summer, concentrate on the deep-water point north of the island.

Area (5) The weedline along the south shoreline attracts muskie, walleye and northern pike. Cast the submerged weed points with deep-diving crankbaits. Backtroll the drop-offs in the 10- to 15-foot depths for summer walleye.

Area (6) This stretch of steep, rocky shoreline is good for walleye. Fish the 10- to 25-foot break using jig and live bait combos. Crankbaits are also productive during summer.

Area (7) Immediately east of Rush Lake, along the south shore, is a small region of weeds that should be fished for walleye and muskie. Work the outside edge in 10 to 13 feet of water.

Area (8) The large bay along the west shoreline has scattered weeds and old fish cribs that hold crappie and largemouth bass. Crappie also relate to the shallow weed edges.

Area (9) This section of north shoreline has a sand bottom and weeds that provide cover for muskie and walleye. The west end of the area is known for producing the best catches. Use your depthfinder to effectively work the available cover.

Area (10) Try twitching floating balsa minnows early in the season along the shoreline weed cover for bass. Plastic worms are more effective in summer.

FISHING TIPS - A variety of structure and depths are present in this premier lake. Weeds, especially cabbage beds, are key areas for walleye, muskie, bass and panfish. Don't overlook the firm bottom found along much of the south shore for summer and fall walleye and muskie. Gravel and rock zones are always important fishing areas.

CONCLUSION - High Lake deserves its reputation for providing quantity and quality fishing. Adequate forage means large gamefish. Besides the well-known walleye and muskie fishery, crappie, perch and largemouth bass are an added feature.

BAMBI LAKE

LOCATION - In the northeast part of the area, just south of Highway B and north of High Lake.

ACCESS - Type IV: To the west side of the lake; this walk-in access is via a logging road taken south off Highway B. It is about 2.5 miles east of the Highway M intersection. The access over state-owned land is difficult to find.

LAKE CHARACTERISTICS
Size and Depth - 13 acres and 19 feet.
Water Source - Seepage lake: No inlet or outlet.
Shoreline - 60% state-owned, the entire west side.
Bottom - 100% muck.
Water - Exceedingly infertile and moderately clear.
Vegetation - Limited to the shoreline zone.

FISHERY
SPECIES - Perch, Bluegill, (Largemouth).
COMMENT - Perch are abundant but stunted.

LAKE MANAGEMENT
Lake Investigation Data - None.
Stocking - None recently.

CONCLUSION - This small, out-of-the-way lake is a typical Northern Wisconsin "pothole." The lack of fertility sharply limits its potential. Currently, perch dominate the fishery to the point where even bluegill are limited.

ELIZABETH LAKE

LOCATION - In the north central part of the section, east of Highway M and about 1 mile northeast of Boulder Junction.

ACCESS - Type IV: On the east end of the lake; this carry-in access is over state-owned land. The shortest portage is through the woods to the west of the High Lake Road/Fishtrap Lake Road intersection. This intersection is 1.2 miles from Highway M on the High-Fishtrap Lake Road.

LAKE CHARACTERISTICS
Size and Depth - 22 acres and 15 feet.
Water Source - Seepage lake: No inlet or outlet.
Shoreline - 25% state-owned, on the southeast side.
Bottom - Primarily muck.

Water - Exceptionally infertile and reasonably clear.
Vegetation - Confined to the shoreline areas.

FISHERY
SPECIES - Perch, Bluegill, (Largemouth Bass), (Crappie).

LAKE MANAGEMENT
Lake Investigation Data - None.
Stocking - None recently.

CONCLUSION - Elizabeth Lake is a small, infertile body of water that cannot sustain a decent fishery. The forage base is inadequate and competition for food is high. Expect slow-growing bluegill and perch. The lack of an established predator species is a serious detriment to the fishery.

MANITOWISH RIVER

LOCATION - Across the entire northern part of the book area; starting at Fishtrap Lake on the east side, it flows west through Boulder Lake, then southwest along Highway H, then back to the northwest below Whitney Lake.

ACCESS
NOTE: Several access points are found on High, Rush and Fishtrap Lakes. See the lake reports for more detailed information.

Type I and III: On the north side of the river; take High-Fishtrap Lake Road (across from Airport Road) for 1.0 mile east of Highway M to the landing sign at Dam Road. Drive east on Dam Road for 0.8 mile down to the dam. There is an unimproved Type I landing on the left and a Type III carry-in landing on the right below the dam. A parking area is directly above the landings. Below the dam, only electric motors are allowed.

Type III: On the north side of the river, at the Highway M bridge, just north of Boulder Junction; there is a short, steep carry-in with limited parking along the road.

Type I: On the west side of the river, just north of Highway K and west of the Highway H intersection; this unimproved beach landing is on Lucas Lane. There is limited parking.

Type III: On the east side of the river on Highway H; it is just south of Rudolph Lake Lane or about 2 miles south of Highway K. There is an unmarked dirt road entrance.

RELATED SERVICES

Boat Rentals - Yes.

Resorts - Yes.

Campgrounds - Yes, at the dam landing. Small individual sites are available on the river.

SPECIAL FEATURES - Well-known as a canoe trip destination, this river has outstanding wilderness aesthetics and wildlife.

RIVER CHARACTERISTICS

Size and Depth - An average of 55 feet wide and 3.5 feet deep.

Water Source - High, Rush and Fishtrap lakes.

Shoreline - 80% publicly owned. Most of it is in natural cover.

Bottom - A gently sloping gradient. Mostly sand and gravel with some muck and rock.

Water - Quite fertile and moderately clear.

Vegetation - Emergent and floating types are abundant in the slower current areas.

FISHERY

SPECIES - Muskie, Walleye, Largemouth Bass, Smallmouth Bass, Northern Pike, Perch, Bluegill, Crappie, Rock Bass, Sucker, Redhorse.

COMMENT - While many species are present, walleye are apparently the most likely fish caught, especially below the Highway K rapids. Otherwise, the flowage stretches hold panfish and the occasional northern, muskie or bass. The state rates this stretch as Class B muskie water.

RIVER MANAGEMENT

River Investigation Data - None.

Stocking - None recently.

FISHING TIPS - Look for walleye in the downstream reaches that are wider and deeper. The deeper holes are important to locate if you want walleye.

The stretch of river down from Fishtrap Lake to the old dam (landing) is a shallow flowage. From the dam to Boulder Lake, the river narrows and fishing pressure is light. Little Rice Lake is fished for muskie, especially early in the season before the weeds take over.

The river down to Highway K offers good fishing for largemouth and panfish. Below Highway K, the river starts out with a quick current over a rock/gravel bottom but slows to a marsh area with a muck bottom.

CONCLUSION - The river provides a beautiful canoe trip. It can also produce a decent walleye, northern, muskie or bass.

SECTION 3

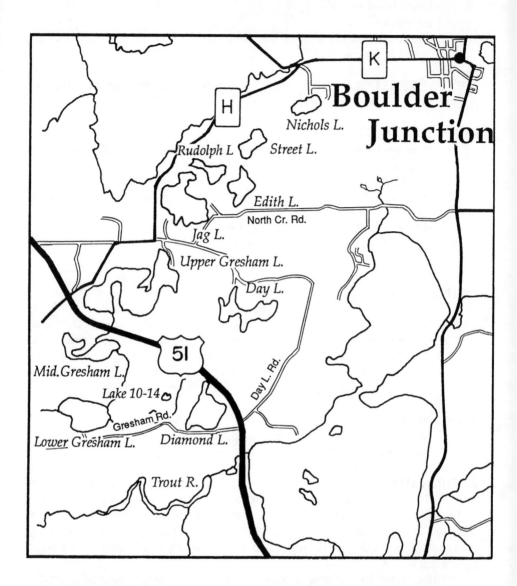

Boulder Junction

K

H

Nichols L.

Rudolph L.   Street L.

Edith L.

North Cr. Rd.

Jag L.

Upper Gresham L.

Day L.

51

Mid. Gresham L.

Lake 10-14

Day L. Rd.

Gresham Rd.

Lower Gresham L.   Diamond L.

Trout R.

Nichols Lake	**Middle Gresham Lake**
Street Lake	**Lower Gresham Lake**
Rudolph Lake	**Day Lake**
Jag Lake	**Lake 10-14**
Edith Lake	**Diamond Lake**
Upper Gresham Lake	**Trout River**

NICHOLS LAKE

LOCATION - In the central part of the area, just south of the Highway H and K intersection, west of Boulder Junction.

ACCESS - Type III: On the east side of the lake; from a marked entrance on Highway H (just south of Highway K), drive 0.7 mile to the landing at the state forest picnic area. There is an easy, but lengthy, carry-in for small boats or canoes. The park has restrooms, picnic facilities, drinking water, and a beach.

RELATED SERVICES
> **Public Parks** - Yes.

SPECIAL FEATURES - Good public use area. Picnicking is popular.

LAKE CHARACTERISTICS
> **Size and Depth** - 40 acres and 16 feet.
> **Water Source** - Seepage lake: No inlet or outlet.
> **Shoreline** - 20% state-owned, entirely on the east end. 20% wetland.
> **Bottom** - 35% sand, 25% gravel, 20% muck, 10% boulder, 10% rubble.
> **Water** - Extremely infertile and fairly clear.
> **Vegetation** - Limited to emergent rushes on the north and west shorelines.

FISHERY
> **SPECIES** - Largemouth Bass, Rock Bass, Bluegill, Perch, Pumpkinseed, Crappie, Sucker, (Smallmouth Bass).
> **COMMENT** - Largemouth bass are sustained by natural reproduction, though they tend to be small. Recently, fishing pressure has removed larger adults, negatively impacting the fishery.

LAKE MANAGEMENT
> **Lake Investigation Data** - None recently.
> **Stocking** - None.

FISHING TIPS - Some old cribs are still a factor in providing fish habitat. Three are along the south shore, two on the north shore and one on the east end. Work close to the available cover for the best action.

CONCLUSION - Nichols Lake is better suited for swimming than fishing, although a few quality bass are present.

STREET LAKE

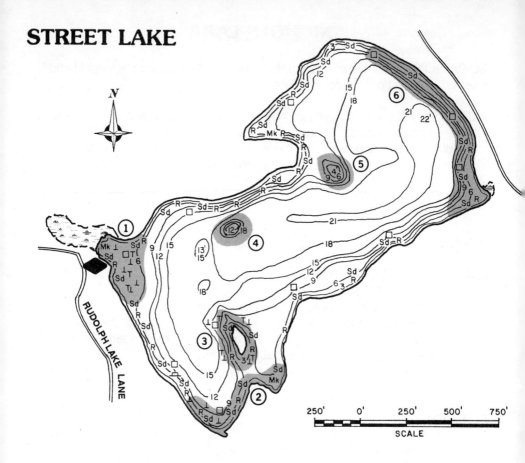

STREET LAKE

LOCATION - In the west central part of the book area, east of Highway H and south of Highway K, southwest of Boulder Junction.

ACCESS - Type I (Public): On the west end of the lake in the small bay; from Highway H (approximately 1.9 miles from the Highway H/K intersection), turn east on Rudolph Lake Lane for 0.6 mile to the access. This is a municipal beach landing with parking. Four-wheel-drive vehicles and small boats are recommended.

SPECIAL FEATURES - Outboard motors are not allowed.

LAKE CHARACTERISTICS
    Size and Depth - 45 acres and 22 feet.
    Water Source - Seepage lake: No inlet or outlet.
    Shoreline - 23% state-owned, entirely on the southeast shore. The island is also state-owned. Almost all of the shoreline is upland.

Bottom - 60% sand, 35% rubble, 5% muck.
Water - Exceptionally infertile and very clear.
Vegetation - Limited to the west end of the lake, primarily emergent and floating varieties. Lily pads and bulrush are scattered along much of the shoreline.

FISHERY
SPECIES
Primary - Largemouth Bass, Perch, Sucker.
Secondary - Northern Pike, Rock Bass, Bluegill.
Limited - Smallmouth Bass.

COMMENT - Largemouth bass are naturally reproducing and are the major gamefish species. Northern pike spawning appears to be non-existent. Fish in the 19- to 24-inch range are present. Bluegill and perch are the most common panfish.

LAKE MANAGEMENT
Lake Investigation Data - None recently.
Stocking - None recently.

LAKE SURVEY MAP - Fishing Areas Shaded
Area (1) Work the weed edges for bluegill and an occasional bass.
Area (2) A thin line of shoreline bulrush and lily pads can provide bass, northern pike and bluegill opportunities.
Area (3) Cast plastic worms along the edge of the lily pads and submergent weeds for bass. Bluegill and a rare pike are also taken.
Area (4) A very small hump is located approximately 140 feet off the north shoreline. Pike, bass and perch relate to this structure, especially during active feeding periods.
Area (5) Northern pike, largemouth bass and perch are found on this small sunken island.
Area (6) Pitch jig n' pigs into the shoreline timber for bass. Bluegill use the shallow cover in the bay.

FISHING TIPS - Down-size your terminal tackle to cope with the clear water. Cast spinnerbaits, floating balsa minnows and in-line spinners for northern pike and bass. Don't overlook the remnants of the old cribs.

CONCLUSION - Street Lake is a fun pothole on which to spend an hour or two on a quiet summer evening. Even though it is not rich in nutrients, it seems to have a fair fish population.

RUDOLPH LAKE

LOCATION - In the west central part of the area, east of and adjacent to Highway H and south of Highway K.

ACCESS - Type III: On the west end of the lake; from Highway H, drive east on an unmarked dirt road for 0.2 mile to the state landing. The road entrance is 0.1 mile south of Rudolph Lake Lane or 2 miles south of Highway K. There is an unimproved, but easy carry-in, with parking for several vehicles.

RELATED SERVICES
Boat Rentals - Yes, at the campground.
Resorts - None.
Campgrounds - Yes, private.

LAKE CHARACTERISTICS
Size and Depth - 39 acres and 24 feet.
Water Source - Seepage lake: No inlet or outlet.
Shoreline - 27% state-owned, the entire east end and a small area at the landing.
Bottom - Mostly muck with minor amounts of sand and gravel.
Water - Extremely infertile and quite clear.
Vegetation - Both emergent and submergent types are present in light to moderate densities.

FISHERY
SPECIES
Primary - Perch, Bluegill, Sunfish, Bullhead.
Secondary - Largemouth Bass.
Limited - (Walleye).
COMMENT - Panfish populations appear to be in control, especially small bluegill and perch. Lake infertility is a limiting factor.

LAKE MANAGEMENT
Lake Investigation Data - None.
Stocking - None recently.

FISHING TIPS - Fish the weed edges or downed shoreline timber and brush. Clear water demands low-light fishing and longer casts in order to be effective.

CONCLUSION - Rudolph Lake's infertility supports a light density of fish, all competing for a limited forage base. However, decent weed cover provides some habitat for panfish and bass. Rudolph yields a few good fish, including an occasional trophy bass.

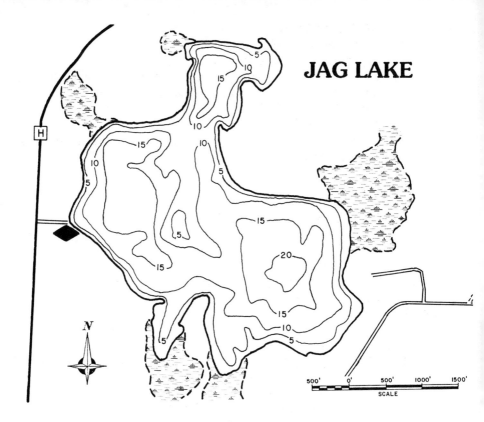

JAG LAKE

LOCATION - In the west central part of the area; just east of Highway H and north of Highway 51.

ACCESS - Type I (Public): On the west side of the lake; from the Highway H/North Creek Road intersection, go north on Highway H for 0.6 mile to a gravel road. Follow this unmarked road east to the access. The landing and parking area are unimproved.

RELATED SERVICES
> **Boat Rentals** - Yes, at resort.
> **Resorts** - Yes.
> **Campgrounds** - Yes, a state-owned juvenile camping facility on the east side.

SPECIAL FEATURES - A fish consumption advisory is in effect for walleye and smallmouth bass.

LAKE CHARACTERISTICS

Size and Depth - 158 acres and 26 feet.

Water Source - Seepage lake: No inlet or outlet.

Shoreline - 73% state-owned, except for the bay on the north end and the northeast side adjacent to the campground. 95% upland.

Bottom - 50% sand, 20% gravel, 20% rock, 10% muck.

Water - Exceedingly infertile and fairly clear.

Vegetation - Floating, emergent and submergent weeds are present mainly in the bays.

FISHERY

SPECIES

Primary - Largemouth Bass, Perch, Rock Bass, Sucker.

Secondary - Smallmouth Bass, Walleye, Bluegill, Crappie, Bullhead.

Limited - Muskie.

COMMENT - Panfish are abundant. However, enough forage exists to allow a portion of the gamefish population to achieve decent size.

FORAGE - Sucker are numerous.

LAKE MANAGEMENT

Lake Investigation Data - An old fyke net and electrofishing survey was conducted to evaluate the fishery .

SPECIES	NUMBER	MAX. SIZE
JAG LAKE COMBINED FYKE NET & ELECTROFISHING SUMMARY		
Walleye	35	27"
Muskie	8	33"
Smallmouth Bass	5	10"
Perch	858	7.5"
Bluegill	199	7.5"
Crappie	114	10"
Rock Bass	113	8"

Stocking - None recently.

Treatment - A total of 46 log cribs were installed in 1967. They are located around the shoreline and across the mouth of the north bay. Five were placed around the island.

FISHING TIPS - Most of the shoreline can be worked for largemouth and smallmouth bass. Downed trees, scattered vegetation and the old cribs all enhance the shoreline zone.

CONCLUSION - Despite the fact that Jag Lake is very infertile, it is large enough to hold good numbers of fish. A trophy bass is a possibility.

EDITH LAKE

LOCATION - In the west central part of the area, east of Highway H and Jag Lake, and south of Highway K.

ACCESS - Type IV: On the west side of the lake; there is a difficult access through the woods from the vicinity of the Jag Lake campground entrance. The south end of the lake adjacent to North Creek Road is privately owned, but the west is entirely public.

LAKE CHARACTERISTICS
> **Size and Depth** - 60 acres and 24 feet.
> **Water Source** - Seepage lake: No inlet or outlet.
> **Shoreline** - 44% state-owned.
> **Bottom** - Sand and gravel, with some rock.
> **Water** - Infertile and very clear.
> **Vegetation** - Limited to a narrow shoreline zone.

FISHERY
> **SPECIES** - Smallmouth Bass, Largemouth Bass, Perch, Bluegill, Pumpkinseed, Sucker, (Crappie).
> **COMMENT** - Smallmouth bass are the only predator species present in any number. Apparently, spawning habitat is excellent for smallmouth. Perch and sucker are numerous.

LAKE MANAGEMENT
> **Lake Investigation Data** - None.
> **Stocking** - None.

CONCLUSION - The infertility of Edith Lake hampers growth rates and suppresses gamefish numbers. However, undersized smallmouth bass are present. Expect abundant, but stunted, perch and bluegill.

UPPER GRESHAM LAKE

LOCATION - In the west central portion of the area, north of, and adjacent to Highway 51, and east of, and adjacent to Highway H.

ACCESS

Type I (Public): On the northeast end of the lake, at the state forest campground; go northeast on Highway H from Highway 51 to North Creek Road. Proceed 0.2 mile east to the marked entrance of the landing and campground.

UPPER GRESHAM LAKE

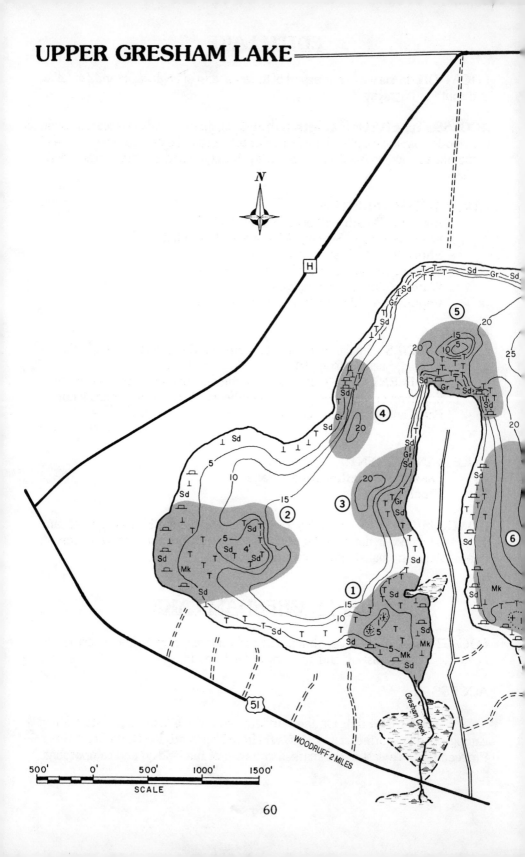

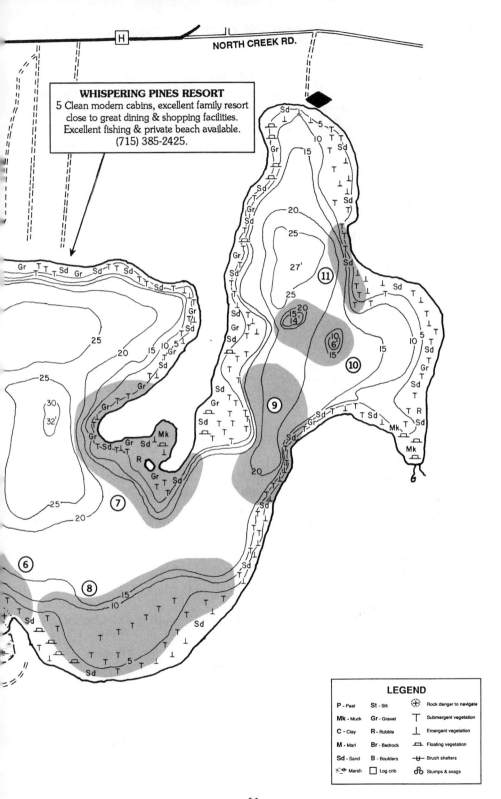

WHISPERING PINES RESORT
5 Clean modern cabins, excellent family resort close to great dining & shopping facilities. Excellent fishing & private beach available. (715) 385-2425.

NORTH CREEK RD.

LEGEND

P - Peat	**St** - Silt	⊕ Rock danger to navigate
Mk - Muck	**Gr** - Gravel	⊤ Submergent vegetation
C - Clay	**R** - Rubble	⊥ Emergent vegetation
M - Marl	**Br** - Bedrock	⚏ Floating vegetation
Sd - Sand	**B** - Boulders	↵ Brush shelters
Marsh	Log crib	⚭ Stumps & snags

61

There is a paved parking area, turn-around, concrete slab ramp and loading pier. Drinking water is available.

Type V: To the southwest end of the lake via the Gresham Creek outlet. There is a Type III access to the creek from Highway 51 about 0.8 mile south of Highway H. Turn off Highway 51 at Harmony Point Road and take the "Old 51" roadbed down to the creek. It is a short, easy carry-in just above the culvert.

RELATED SERVICES
Boat Rentals - Yes.
Resorts - Yes.
Campgrounds - Yes, state-owned on northeast end.

LAKE CHARACTERISTICS
Size and Depth - 375 acres and 32 feet.
Water Source - Drained lake: An outlet (Gresham Creek) on the southwest end to Middle Gresham Lake. No inlets but several springs.
Shoreline - 57% state-owned, except for the south side and a portion of the north shore.
Bottom - 60% sand, 25% muck, 10% gravel, 5% rubble.
Water - Quite fertile and slightly murky.
Vegetation - Abundant weed growth is found in the shoreline areas. Emergent, submergent and floating varieties are present. Much of the vegetation extends 100 to 300 feet from shore, especially on the points.

FISHERY
SPECIES
Primary - Walleye, Muskie, Northern Pike, Bluegill, Crappie.
Secondary - Largemouth Bass, Rock Bass, Pumpkinseed.
Limited - Smallmouth Bass.
COMMENT - Upper Gresham Lake is highly productive for a variety of species as good weed cover, forage and fertility are available. Walleye are the dominant gamefish, but are sustained by state stocking. Panfish appear to be slow growing and abundant.

LAKE MANAGEMENT
Lake Investigation Data - An electrofishing survey looked at walleye natural reproduction. Only a few young-of-the-year fish were seen, confirming that only minimal reproduction is occurring. The study concluded with a recommendation to continue walleye stocking (see chart on top of next page).

UPPER GRESHAM LAKE ELECTROFISHING SUMMARY		
SPECIES	**NUMBER**	**MAX. SIZE**
Walleye	46	22"
Largemouth Bass	6	14.5"
Smallmouth Bass	2	10.5"
Muskie	2	16"

Stocking

UPPER GRESHAM LAKE STOCKING SUMMARY			
YEAR	**SPECIES**	**NUMBER**	**SIZE**
1984	Walleye	19,000	3"
1985	Muskie	700	12"
1986	Walleye	19,000	3"
1987	Muskie	700	8"
1988	Walleye	19,000	Fingerling
1989	Muskie	338	10"
1990	Walleye	18,900	Fingerling

LAKE SURVEY MAP - Fishing Areas Shaded

Area (1) The weedy outlet bay of Gresham Creek yields northern pike and muskie. Work the deeper weed edges with in-line spinners. Panfish relate to the thicker weed cover.

Area (2) Northern pike and muskie use the shallow sand bar and abundant weed cover of the west bay. Cast surface lures over the cabbage and coontail beds.

Area (3) Backtroll the 10- to 15-foot weedline along this gravel point for walleye. Largemouth bass relate to the edges of the shallow weeds. On bright days, cast back into the weeds for bass.

Area (4) Walleye fishing along this deep weedline can be excellent during summer. If action is slow, try working the deeper water. Largemouth bass are found primarily in the shallow weed growth along shore.

Area (5) The steep shoreline breaks and well-defined weedline attract walleye and muskie to this point. Deep weed edges are key, especially when working the small submerged island.

Area (6) The weedline and the 10- to 15-foot depths provide walleye, muskie and northern pike action. Slop fishing techniques for bass are effective in the southern bay and along shoreline cover.

Area (7) This point offers steep shoreline breaks and a variety of weed cover. Walleye, muskie and bass relate to the deep cabbage beds. Look for suspended fish, especially muskie, off the point.

Area (8) The shoreline weeds offer good action for bass and panfish. The deeper cabbage beds, found at the 10- to 12- foot depths, produce walleye, muskie and northern pike.

Area (9) The Narrows have an interesting combination of weeds and good drop-offs. Walleye usually are found on the deep, secondary breaks and along the channel. Fish the edge of the cabbage along the west side for muskie and pike.

Area (10) Work the two small underwater islands for walleye and muskie. The shallower east island has better muskie habitat than the hump on the west side. Deep-running crankbaits are recommended for muskie, while vertical presentations are good for walleye.

Area (11) Walleye are found on the deep breaklines, especially those close to the weed edge. Use your depthfinder to locate these critical weed breaks.

FISHING TIPS - Upper Gresham Lake is relatively easy to fish by using weedline techniques and presentations. Much of the shoreline can be worked for gamefish and panfish. Choose areas with a well-defined weed edge adjacent to deep water. Inside turns or submerged weed points are always good bets. The murky water calls for bright colors, in everything from walleye jigs to muskie bucktails. Floating balsa minnows "twitched" slowly over the weed tops are a good bet for early spring pike and bass. Remember, in most cases, the shoreline zone is the area to work as much of the midlake bottom is very flat.

CONCLUSION - This lake offers decent fishing for gamefish and abundant panfish. Although they are typically small, the perch and bluegill are usually cooperative. However, Upper Gresham Lake receives moderate to heavy fishing pressure.

MIDDLE GRESHAM LAKE

LOCATION - In the west central part of the book area, south of Highway 51 and east of Highway H.

ACCESS - Type V: To the northeast side of the lake, via the Gresham Creek inlet; there is a Type III access to the creek from Highway 51, about 0.8 mile south of Highway H. Turn off Highway 51 at Harmony Point Road, and take the "Old 51" roadbed down to the creek. It is a short, easy carry-in above the culvert.

RELATED SERVICES
    Boat Rentals - Yes.
    Resorts - Yes.
    Campgrounds - None.

LAKE CHARACTERISTICS
    Size and Depth - 53 acres and 17 feet.
    Water Source - Drainage lake: An inlet on the northeast side (Gresham Creek) from Upper Gresham Lake and an outlet on the east end (Gresham Creek) to Lower Gresham Lake.

Shoreline - 80% state-owned, except for the north side of the west lake and the north side of the east lake.

Bottom - Mostly muck with some sand and gravel.

Water - Moderately fertile and fairly clear.

Vegetation - Abundant weeds dominate the entire lake, leaving only a small open channel by midsummer. Algae bloom occurs annually.

FISHERY
SPECIES
Primary - Northern Pike, Muskie, Perch, Bluegill.

Secondary - Largemouth Bass, Crappie, Bullhead, Pumpkinseed.

Limited - Walleye.

COMMENT - Panfish numbers, chiefly perch and bluegill, remain in control of this fishery despite state attempts to change the predator/prey balance. The heavy weed growth impedes predators from utilizing the prey species. This results in abundant and stunted panfish.

LAKE MANAGEMENT
Lake Investigation Data - None recently.

Stocking - None recently.

FISHING TIPS - Weed fishing expertise is required as the weeds literally choke the lake by summer. Fish early in the season before the weeds take over. Muskie and panfish are the best bets, although at times, northern pike angling is excellent.

CONCLUSION - Middle Gresham, despite its proximity to Highway 51, receives little fishing pressure, largely due to lack of adequate public access.

LOWER GRESHAM LAKE

LOCATION - In the west central part of the area, south of Highway 51 and east of Highway H.

ACCESS

Type I (Private): On the south side of the lake; from Highway 51, proceed west 2.3 miles on Gresham Road to Popes Road. Turn north for 0.3 mile to the unimproved access.

Type V: To the west end of the lake via the Gresham Creek outlet; there is Type III access to the creek at the Highway H culvert which is ½ mile north of Gresham Road. There is parking along the road.

LAKE CHARACTERISTICS

Size and Depth - 149 acres and 12 feet.

Water Source - Drainage lake: Gresham Creek inlets on the northeast side and outlets on the west end. Both the inlet and outlet are considered navigable.

Shoreline - Mostly upland.

Bottom - Primarily sand, with some areas of muck and gravel.

Water - Slightly fertile and moderately clear.

Vegetation - Submergent varieties are abundant, primarily cabbage and coontail. Emergent types (bulrush) line much of the shoreline.

RELATED SERVICES

Boat Rentals - Yes, at resort.

Resorts - Yes.

Campgrounds - None.

FISHERY

SPECIES

Primary - Northern Pike, Muskie, Bluegill, Perch, Sucker.

Secondary - Largemouth Bass, Crappie, Rock Bass, Bullhead, Pumpkinseed.

Limited - Walleye.

COMMENT - Gamefish populations in recent years have had a slight impact on the abundant panfish. Bluegill, perch and pumpkinseed are the primary panfish species. Muskie are stocked in an effort to control panfish.

LAKE MANAGEMENT

Lake Investigation Data - None recently.

Stocking

LOWER GRESHAM LAKE STOCKING SUMMARY			
YEAR	SPECIES	NUMBER	SIZE
1983	Muskie	300	9"
1985	Walleye	7,000	3"
1990	Muskie	300	Fingerling

FISHING TIPS - This lake offers decent angling, especially early in the season. Cabbage weeds are in excellent supply throughout the lake and offer good pike and muskie fishing.

Select hot colors, such as fluorescent orange, green and red for the murky water. Use the same colors for walleye jigging. Despite the dark water, black bucktails are a local muskie favorite.

CONCLUSION - Lower Gresham Lake is a good choice if action is the goal, but expect mostly small pike.

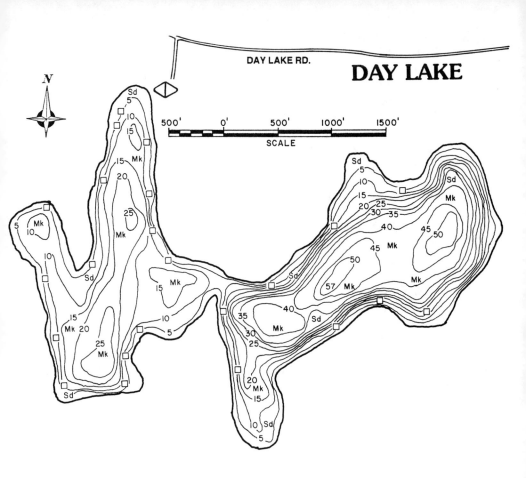

DAY LAKE

LOCATION - In the west central part of the area, northeast of Highway 51, and west of Trout Lake.

ACCESS - Type III: On the north end of the west lake; from Highway 51, take Day Lake Road north for 3.5 miles to a sand beach landing and unimproved parking area.

RELATED SERVICES
    Boat Rentals - None.
    Resorts - None.
    Campgrounds - Yes, two state wilderness campsites are on the lake.

SPECIAL FEATURES - Outboard motors are prohibited.

LAKE CHARACTERISTICS

Size and Depth - 117 acres and 57 feet.

Water Source - Seepage lake: No inlet or outlet, but several small springs are present.

Shoreline - 100% state-owned; entirely upland.

Bottom - 80% sand, 20% gravel.

Water - Extremely infertile and quite clear.

Vegetation - Very sparse; limited to a narrow shoreline fringe.

FISHERY

SPECIES - Largemouth Bass, Bluegill, Pumpkinseed, Perch, Bullhead, Sucker.

COMMENT - Panfish numbers are high, but they are small in size. Largemouth bass are small and display slow growth rates. Most of the bass present are below 10.5 inches.

LAKE MANAGEMENT

Lake Investigation Data - None recently.

Stocking - None.

Treatment - In 1968, 25 fish shelters were installed along the shoreline.

FISHING TIPS - Fish the old brush shelters and submerged timber on the shallow west end of the lake. Work the 3- to 20-foot depths at the east end for bass and bluegill. Expect very little in quality, but occasionally a bass up to 5 pounds is taken.

CONCLUSION - Day Lake is beautiful water to be on, but not necessarily a good choice for catching quality fish. The lack of an adequate forage base and extreme infertility severely limits its potential.

LAKE 10-14 (UNNAMED)

LOCATION - In the west central part of the book area, southwest of Highway 51, west of Diamond Lake, and north of Gresham Road.

ACCESS - Type III: On the north side of the lake; from Highway 51 (about ½ mile northwest of the Diamond Lake Wayside), turn south on an unmarked road through the woods for about 0.7 mile to the access.

LAKE CHARACTERISTICS

Size and Depth - 9 acres and 20 feet.

Water Source - Seepage lake: No inlet or outlet.

Shoreline - 100% state-owned. A floating bog surrounds the lake.

Bottom - Mostly muck with some sand.

Water - Very infertile and moderately clear.

Vegetation - Extremely limited.

FISHERY
SPECIES - Largemouth Bass, Bluegill, (Smallmouth Bass).
COMMENT - Bluegill are abundant and small in size though a few are present up to 7 inches. Largemouth bass display slow growth rates, with few fish exceeding 15 inches.

LAKE MANAGEMENT
Lake Investigation Data - None recently.
Stocking - None.

FISHING TIPS - Lake 10-14 is a small wilderness "pothole" that offers good depth. It is fished quite regularly for its small size and location, especially for bluegill. Bass fishing must be confined to the edge, as fish relate to the narrow bog fringe, especially on bright sunny days. Always work any available structure such as, downed trees, brush and bog points. A quality fish is a rare possibility.

DIAMOND LAKE

LOCATION - In the west central part of the area, west of, and adjacent to Highway 51.

ACCESS - Type I (Public): On the north end of the lake; this marked wayside is adjacent to Highway 51. There is a paved parking area and concrete ramp.

RELATED SERVICES
Boat Rentals - None.
Resorts - None.
Campgrounds - None.
Public Parks - Yes, a wayside with restrooms and drinking water.

LAKE CHARACTERISTICS
Size and Depth - 122 acres and 40 feet.
Water Source - Seepage lake: No inlet or outlet.
Shoreline - 40% state-owned; the entire north end.
Bottom - 90% sand, 10% gravel.
Water - Extremely infertile and very clear. Oxygen levels are adequate at all depths.
Vegetation - Extremely scarce, usually confined to a narrow shoreline zone, and are typically emergent.

FISHERY
SPECIES
Primary - Smallmouth Bass, Largemouth Bass, Perch, Rock Bass.
Secondary - Walleye, Muskie, Pumpkinseed, Bluegill.
Limited - Crappie.

DIAMOND LAKE

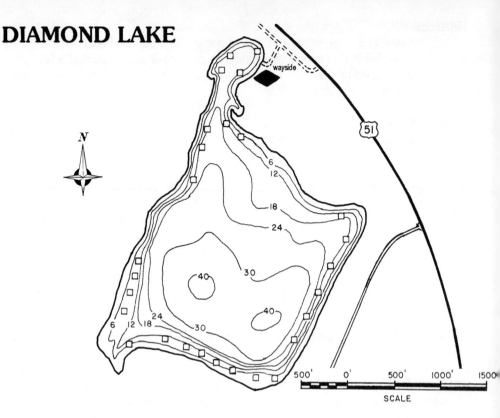

COMMENT - Diamond Lake's dramatic infertility limits the fishery. Largemouth and smallmouth bass are the primary gamefish and show below average growth rates. Muskie and walleye are present but are difficult to locate. Perch and rock bass are numerous, though of small average size.

LAKE MANAGEMENT
    Lake Investigation Data - None recently.
    Stocking - None recently.
    Treatment - Forty-eight log fish shelters were installed along the shoreline from 1956 through 1967. Those placed in 1967 are along the east and south shores, the lower west shore and the entire north bay.

FISHING TIPS - Diamond Lake, though fairly small in size, is surprisingly difficult to fish. Concentrate on the steeper shoreline drop-offs on the east and west sides. The old cribs and shoreline drowned wood provide the best habitat, especially when adjacent to deep water. Water clarity demands down-sized terminal tackle and light monofilament.

CONCLUSION - This water is very infertile, despite its size. Forage is at a minimum resulting, in few fish and small average size. Spend your time accordingly.

TROUT RIVER

LOCATION - In the southwestern part of the area, starting as an outlet from Trout Lake on the west side of the south basin, and flowing to the west.

ACCESS - Type III: On the north side of the river; from Highway 51, turn west on Gresham Road for 2.3 miles. There is an unmarked gravel road opposite Popes Road. Follow this unmarked road to the access. The road is in good condition and there is ample parking. It is a short, easy carry-in to the river.

RELATED SERVICES
Boat Rentals - None.
Resorts - None.
Campgrounds - Yes, an overnight spot at landing.
Public Park - Yes, a picnic area at the landing.

SPECIAL FEATURES - A popular river for canoe trips.

RIVER CHARACTERISTICS
Size and Depth - This section is approximately 4 miles long, 3½ feet deep, and has an average width of 30-feet.
Water Source - Trout Lake (flows into the Manitowish Chain).
Shoreline - State-owned, except for the first 1½ miles which run through the Trout Lake golf course.
Bottom - 50% muck, 45% sand, 5% gravel.
Water - Highly fertile and clear.
Vegetation - Both emergent and submergent varieties are available, especially in the slower current areas.

FISHERY
SPECIES - Muskie, Northern Pike, Walleye, Largemouth Bass, Smallmouth Bass, Bluegill, Rock Bass, Perch, Pumpkinseed.
COMMENT - The state rates it as a Class A muskie river. Walleye are present in minor numbers.

FISHING TIPS - Work the deeper holes on the bends. Weedbeds next to deep water must not be overlooked. Shoreline rocks, downed trees and brush create current breaks that hold fish.

CONCLUSION - The Trout River offers a pleasant interlude for those who enjoy a quite canoe trip. The wilderness aesthetics are nice, and the fishing provides reasonable variety.

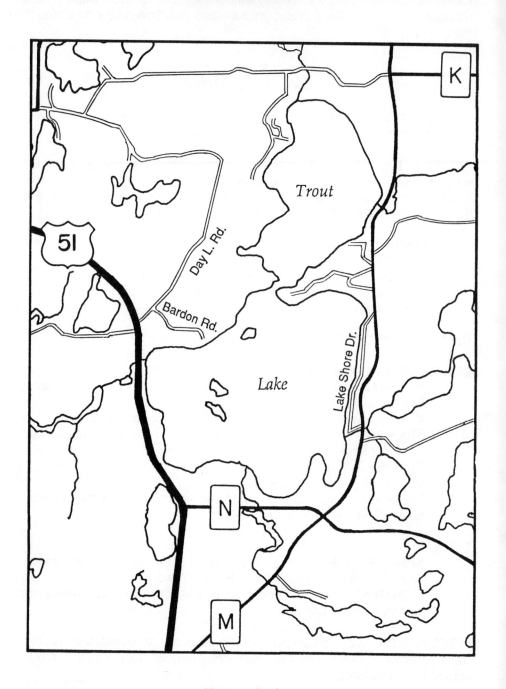

Trout Lake

TROUT LAKE

LOCATION - In the south central part of the area, east of Highway 51, north of Highway N, and west of Highway M.

ACCESS

A **Type III (Public):** On the northwest side of south lake; from Highway 51, take Day Lake Road north for 0.3 mile to Bardon Road. Turn right and continue for 0.7 mile to where the road ends and a logging road begins. Approximately 500 feet down this road, take the right fork for 0.2 mile to the landing. This steep, gravel ramp is not recommended for larger rigs. Turn-around room is limited.

B **Type I (Public):** On the east side of the south lake; from Highway M, turn west on Lake Shore Drive for 0.2 mile. Proceed left a short distance to the landing which is part of a state forest campground. There is a paved parking area, turn-around, concrete ramp and loading pier.

C **Type III (Public):** On the east side of south lake; from Highway M, turn west on Lake Shore Drive for 0.9 mile. There is an easy carry-in to a beach with roadside parking.

D **Type II (Public):** At the northeast corner of south lake; from Highway M, turn west at the north end of Lake Shore Drive to this unimproved facility. A gravel ramp and limited parking are found.

E **Type I (Public):** On the northeast side of north lake within the state forest campground; this facility is adjacent to Highway M on the west side of the road. This quality access has a concrete ramp, loading pier and ample parking. A campground, picnic area and beach are included.

RELATED SERVICES

    Boat Rentals - Yes.

    Resorts - Yes.

    Campgrounds - Yes, two campgrounds on the east side and several wilderness sites on the west side and on the islands near the narrows.

    Public Parks - Yes, the Trout Lake Point Picnic Area is at the end of the Forestry Headquarters Road.

    Bait Shops - Yes, several in Boulder Junction.

    Guide Services - Yes, in Boulder Junction.

SPECIAL FEATURES - Trout Lake is one of Northern Wisconsin's most beautiful and challenging fishing waters. It has excellent public use facilities and recreational opportunities.

    Lake trout fishing is closed from Cathedral Point south throughout south lake.

A consumption advisory exists for walleye over 18 inches, including a recommendation of no consumption of walleye over 22 inches.

Caution is urged while navigating on Trout Lake, especially on the south lake. Shallow rock and gravel bars can be difficult to detect.

LAKE CHARACTERISTICS

Size and Depth - 3,870 acres and 115 feet.

Water Source - Drainage lake: Inlets from North Creek, Allequash Creek, Mann Creek and Stevenson Creek. An outlet on the west side of the south lake to Trout River.

Shoreline - 85% state-owned, except for the north and northwest shore of north lake, and the south and west shore of the south lake.

Bottom - Mostly sand and gravel with rock and some muck.

Water - Quite fertile and very clear.

Vegetation - Light to moderate, mostly cabbage and shoreline lily pads. Other varieties present include wild celery, coontail, milfoil, bulrush and spikerush.

FISHERY

SPECIES

Primary - Walleye, Muskie, Smallmouth Bass, Northern Pike, Rock Bass, Perch, Cisco.

Secondary - Lake Trout, Largemouth Bass, Whitefish, Crappie, Burbot.

Limited - Pumpkinseed, Bluegill, (Brook Trout).

COMMENT - Northern pike are apparently expanding their numbers. Walleye have moved back into a primary status due to a recent stocking program that was initiated to offset minimal natural reproduction. Brook trout have moved at times into the lake from feeder streams.

Trout Lake is famous for its trophy muskie, as it continues to produce fish in the 40-pound class. A rich diet of cisco and whitefish contributes to the trophy potential of this water.

FORAGE - A large variety of minnows, including shiners and dace are present. Cisco and whitefish are important deep water food sources for walleye, muskie, northern pike and lake trout. Also, three species of crayfish, including Rusty crayfish are present.

LAKE MANAGEMENT

Lake Investigation Data - During the period from 1971 to 1982, few walleye were stocked and their numbers declined dramatically. Since 1983, walleye stocking has resumed. Electrofishing surveys indicate all stockings established significant year classes except 1984, when smaller-sized fingerling were stocked. The population estimate from the 1988 spring fyke net survey indicated a low walleye population of 1.5 fish/acre (see chart at top of next page).

TROUT LAKE SPRING WALLEYE FYKE NET SUMMARY		
SPECIES	**SIZE (in inches)**	**NUMBER**
Walleye	Less than 12.0	50
Walleye	12.0 - 14.9	1,022
Walleye	15.0 - 17.9	789
Walleye	18.0 - 20.9	221
Walleye	21.0 - 23.9	173
Walleye	24.0 - 26.9	88
Walleye	27.0 - 29.9	102
Walleye	30.0 - 32.9	14

Additionally, Trout Lake's famous lake trout fishery has become the focus of concern. Dramatic declines in the trout population have been occurring, and adult trout have decreased in average size.

Stocking

TROUT LAKE STOCKING SUMMARY			
YEAR	**SPECIES**	**NUMBER**	**SIZE**
1983	Walleye	66,000	3"
	Lake Trout	19,000	8"
1984	Walleye	101,000	Fingerling
	Lake Trout	20,000	Yearling
1985	Muskie	110	Fingerling
	Walleye	132,800	Fingerling
	Lake Trout	15,600	Yearling
1986	Muskie	900	--
	Walleye	152,100	Fingerling
	Lake Trout	4,700	Yearling
1987	Walleye	100,000	3"
	Lake Trout	50,000	Fingerling
1988	Muskie	2,155	Fingerling
	Walleye	100,980	Fingerling
1989	Walleye	186,780	Fingerling
	Walleye	650,000	Fry
1990	Muskie	1,880	Fingerling
	Walleye	48,360	Fry
	Walleye	51,060	Fingerling

LAKE SURVEY MAP - Fishing Areas Shaded

Area (1) Work the line of bulrushes and the deeper submergent weeds along Kerns Point for pike, muskie and the occasional walleye. Pay close attention to the 20- to 30-foot depths in May and June for all three species.

Area (2) A large sandbar on the northeast shore, between the public campgrounds and the private camp, can hold evening walleye early in the season. Old

SOUTH TROUT LAKE

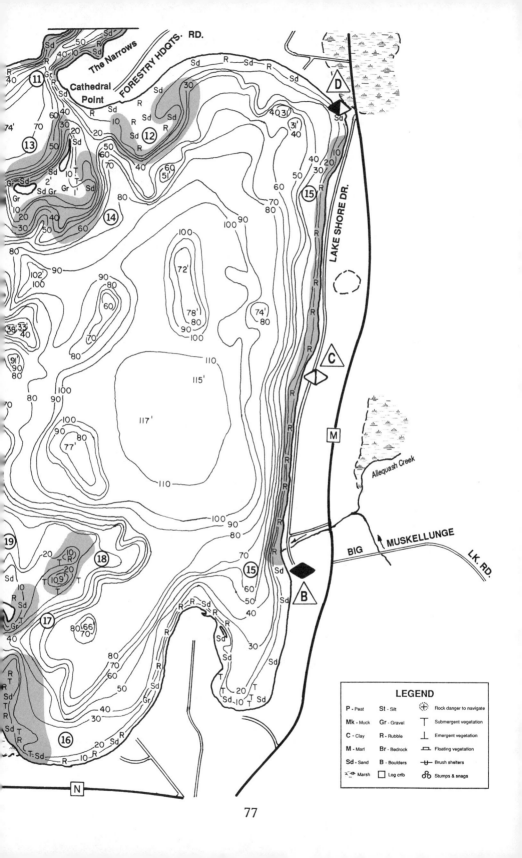

fish shelters in the 12-foot depths may still attract walleye and panfish.

Area (3) Stevenson Creek inlet draws early season walleye. This area is best during periods of increased current flow. Work this spot in evening for muskie.

Area (4) Four underwater islands top off at 42 to 62 feet deep. Lake trout tend to relate to the edges, especially in May and June. Walleye anglers use large redtail chubs in midsummer to take trophies.

Area (5) Work the deeper edges of the emergent rushes and adjacent submergent weeds for muskie, walleye, northern pike and an occasional bass.

Area (6) A 12-foot deep rock bar offers walleye and smallmouth possibilities. Cast the shoreline drop-off at the 10- to 20-foot depths for evening muskie.

Area (7) Fish the mouth of the small weedy bay for northern pike and muskie. Pay special attention to deeper weed edges. When casting, be sure to work parallel to the weedline whenever possible.

Area (8) Drop-offs around the small island are used by walleye and smallmouth bass, especially on the east and south side. Muskie relate to the 15-foot deep saddle between shore and the island.

Area (9) Muskie anglers drift or use an electric motor to parallel cast the rocky, steep breaks with deep-running crankbaits, jerkbaits or weighted bucktails. This area produces best in September and October. Walleye relate to the inside turns of the drop-off around the point at the south end of the area.

Area (10) The 8-foot deep bar, north of the narrows, is popular with walleye anglers. Backtroll the steep edges of the bar with Lindy-Rigs tipped with live bait. A few muskie are also taken.

Area (11) Both shorelines of the narrows have deep breaklines that hold smallmouth, muskie and walleye. Probe the 10- to 40-foot depths with live bait rigs. The small bay on the west side has also produced quality catches.

Area (12) Walleye, smallmouth bass and panfish use the sand/gravel bar south of Cathedral Point. Backtroll the edges of this large, flat bar with jig/live bait combos. Generally, the 10- to 40-foot depths yield the best results.

Area (13) Work the steep drop-off north of Fisk Island and Campsite Island for walleye. Jigs tipped with minnows are popular in May and June, while leeches and nightcrawlers are preferred from mid-June through August.

Area (14) The large sand/gravel bar south of Fisk Island attracts walleye and the occasional muskie, especially late in the day. Concentrate on the edges of the bar. Be aware of very shallow water near the islands.

Area (15) Smallmouth bass and walleye are found along the rubble bottom of the steep east shoreline. The remnants of some old fish cribs may still be a factor, particularly in the northern part of this area.

Area (16) South of Miller Island is a shallow underwater point and weedy flat that yield muskie and northern pike. Fish the 20- to 30- foot depths along the edges of the point for walleye.

Area (17) Muskie often relate to the excellent bottom structure adjacent to the south and east sides of Miller Island.

Area (18) Two relatively small bars rise to within 8 and 9 feet of the surface and offer muskie and walleye fishing. Submerged vegetation and the deep secondary break nearby often produce the best action.

NORTH TROUT LAKE

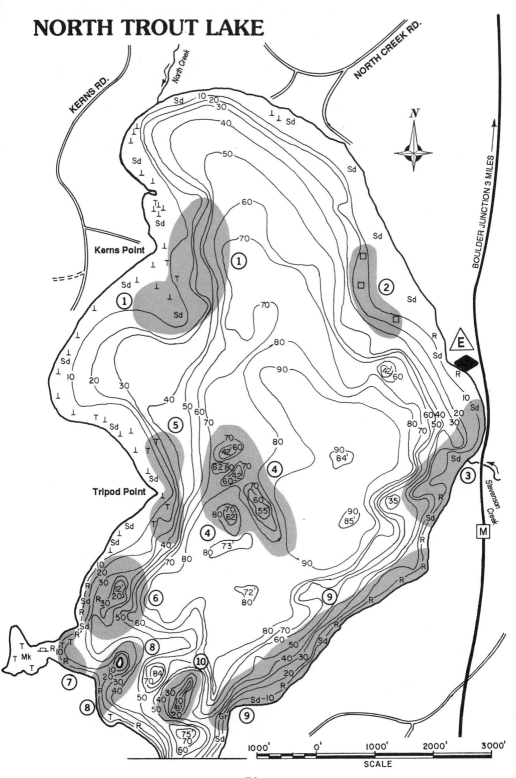

Area (19) Between Miller Island and Haunted Island are several underwater humps that offer walleye, muskie and northern pike. Drift and cast deep-diving crankbaits over the 7- to 30-foot depths.

Area (20) Old brush shelters on the north side of Zimmerman Island and the south side of Haunted Island may still harbor walleye, smallmouth bass, muskie and rock bass. The shallow water around the islands offers a variety of bottom structure that produces walleye and muskie. The 10- to 20- foot depths between the two islands are popular areas for walleye and muskie anglers.

Area (21) Muskie and walleye use the circular, 7-foot deep, sunken island and the shallow submerged bar to the west.

Area (22) This section of the west shoreline has a number of submerged bars, underwater points and bays that are inhabited by smallmouth bass, walleye, muskie and panfish. A depthfinder is useful for locating and working the drop-offs. Old fish shelters placed in 10 to 15 feet of water still hold a few fish.

Area (23) These two bars are only 6 to 7 feet deep and are extensions of shoreline structure. Muskie are the main attraction, especially in evening or during low light conditions. Work the deeper sides for walleye. Both of these structures can be fished by drifting with a west or northwest wind.

Area (24) Both of these offshore humps offer walleye fishing. Use a depthfinder to locate these key structures.

FISHING TIPS - Fishing Trout Lake is a challenge and warrants consideration of hiring a guide. A depthfinder is absolutely necessary, since bottom structure varies dramatically. This is water to develop your own fishing patterns as dozens of underwater points, submerged islands, reefs, rock bars and edges are available for discovery.

Walleye anglers know that depth is an important component to success. Concentrate on the 10- to 30-foot depths from late May to early June. Summer walleye are typically found in the 15- to 40-foot range. Late evening or night fishing the subtle humps is a key to big walleye in summer and fall. Those working for trophies, should stick to large chubs at least 4- to 5-inches long.

The lake deserves its reputation for trophy muskie, as fish up to 40 pounds have been caught. Big baits are the norm. Large jerkbaits in the Eddie and Smity tradition along with big bucktails are highly recommended. Black, natural and yellow colors are local favorites. Deep-running crankbaits are important for working the sharp drop-offs. Weighting bucktails or jerkbaits is also a good tip.

Muskie often suspend in summer and deep fishing is usually a must. However, large fish have been taken on surface lures or bucktails during the summer evening hours over relatively shallow structure.

In late fall, anglers using large suckers on quick strike rigs are usually successful. Generally, the 20- to 50-depths produce the best action. Pike seem to be increasing in number, and along with smallmouth bass are underfished. Northern of excellent size are a distinct possibility.

SECTION 5

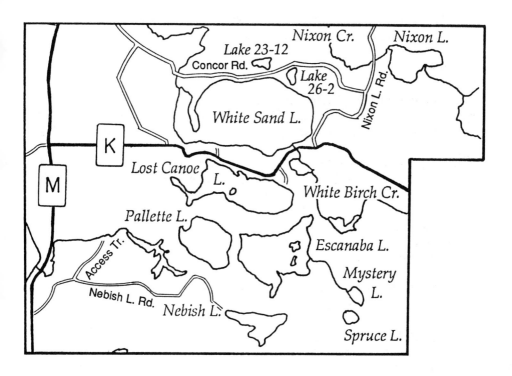

White Sand Lake   **Pallette Lake**
Lake 23-12 (Unnamed)   **Escanaba Lake**
Lake 26-2 (Nellie L.)   **Nebish Lake**
Nixon Lake   **Mystery Lake**
Lost Canoe Lake   **Spruce Lake**
Stevenson Springs

WHITE SAND LAKE

LOCATION - In the east central part of the area, just north of Highway K and east of Highway M and Boulder Junction.

ACCESS

A **Type I (Public):** On the southeast side of the lake; this site is adjacent to Highway K, just west of White Birch Creek. There is a small, unimproved parking area, concrete slab ramp and loading pier. A shallow sand beach is also available.

B **Type III (Public):** On the north side of the lake, take Old K Road north of Highway K to Concora Road. Turn right and follow Concora Road to the south. Continue east on a logging road to the state-owned land.

RELATED SERVICES

Boat Rentals - Yes, at the resort.
Resorts - Yes.
Campgrounds - None.
Public Parks - Yes, nearby at the wayside 0.1 mile west of Access A with picnic area, drinking water and restrooms.

LAKE CHARACTERISTICS

Size and Depth - 728 acres and 68 feet.
Water Source - Drainage lake: An inlet on the southeast end from White Birch Creek and an outlet on the west end to White Sand Creek and the Manitowish River.
Shoreline - 55% state-owned; the entire east half of the lake and the west side of the outlet bay, except at the creek.
Bottom - 40% sand, 40% gravel, 10% muck (only in the shallow outlet bay), and 10% rock. The bottom is steeply sloped around the east half of the lake.
Water - Slightly fertile and very clear.
Vegetation - Submergent and emergent types are present. Portions of the shoreline are lined with rushes. Deep submergent vegetation is located in the west bay.

FISHERY

SPECIES
Primary - Muskie, Smallmouth Bass, Rock Bass, Perch, Cisco.
Secondary - Walleye, Northern Pike, Crappie, Pumpkinseed.
Limited - Largemouth Bass, Bluegill.
COMMENT - Muskie, smallmouth bass and walleye are the significant predator species. The trophy potential for both walleye and muskie is excellent because cisco provide superb forage for larger fish. Additionally,

a decent smallmouth bass population is available, including large fish.

Walleye are largely sustained by state stocking programs. Limited natural reproduction of walleye is occurring. Both bass species are naturally reproducing.

LAKE MANAGEMENT

Lake Investigation Data - A recent spring fyke net survey assessed the walleye fishery and determined the effects of stocking. As a result of the study, the DNR has estimated the adult walleye population to be 1,755 or 2.4 fish per acre. The fyke net captured 17 walleye between 28 and 29 inches.

WHITE SAND LAKE FYKE NET SUMMARY		
SPECIES	SIZE RANGE	NUMBER
Walleye	9.5" - 14.9"	633
Walleye	15.0" - 19.9"	84
Walleye	20" - 29"	106

Stocking

WHITE SAND LAKE STOCKING SUMMARY			
YEAR	SPECIES	NUMBER	SIZE
1984	Walleye	31,000	3"
1986	Walleye	36,000	3"
1987	Muskie	700	11"
1988	Walleye	34,560	Fingerling
1990	Walleye	42,084	Fingerling

Treatment - Old fish cribs were once a significant factor in concentrating fish. Expect them to be less important after this period of time due to deterioration. However, even a crib remnant can hold a few fish.

LAKE SURVEY MAP - Fishing Areas Shaded

Area (1) The east shore has a long bar that rises to within 10 feet of the surface. Use a depthfinder to locate the deep edges and slowly backtroll live bait rigs for walleye. The bar has scattered weeds and a sand/gravel bottom that attract walleye and muskie. Deep-running crankbaits, jig/live bait combos and slip bobbers can all produce.

Area (2) Smallmouth bass and walleye use the rocky habitat along the south shoreline throughout the year. In early spring, the bay just west of the White Birch Creek inlet is used by spawning walleye. Jig and live bait combos are preferred for working this rocky structure. The steep shoreline breaks also yield late fall muskie. A depthfinder is a valuable tool in locating and fishing the changes in depth and bottom composition.

Area (3) The mouth of the west bay provides good spring action for walleye, muskie and perhaps northern pike.

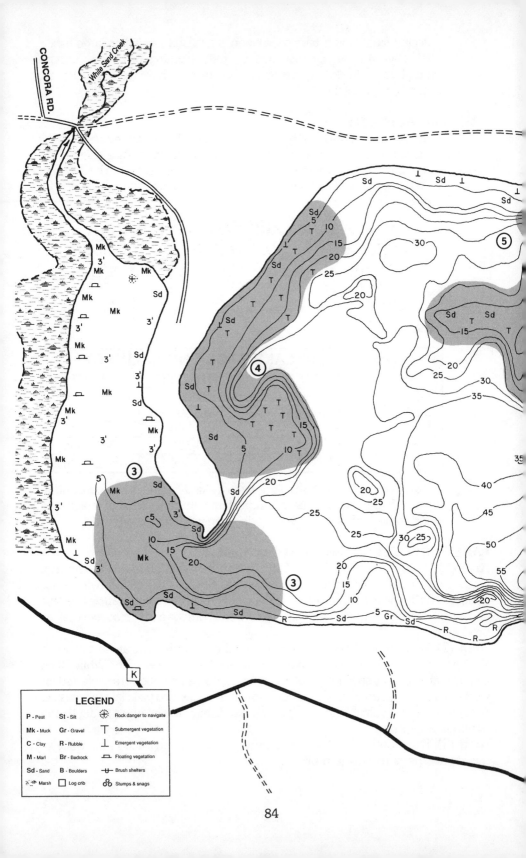

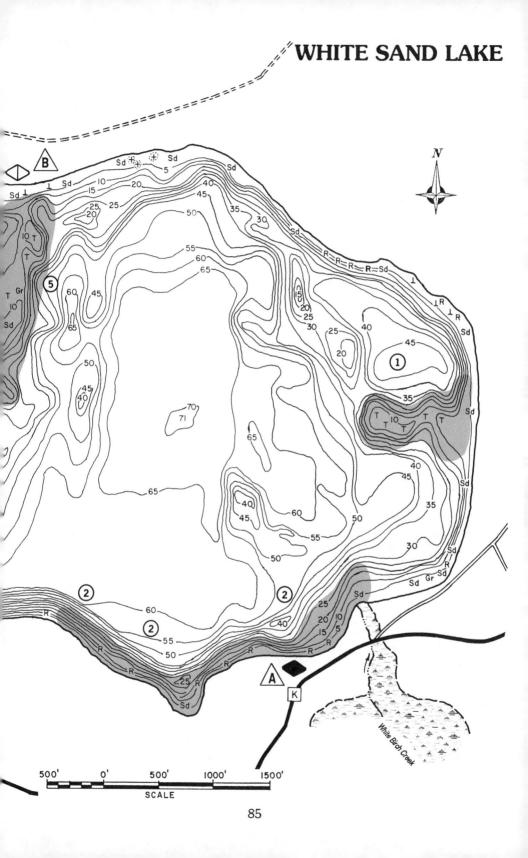

WHITE SAND LAKE

Area (4) A series of cribs in combination with submergent weed patches offer muskie, walleye, smallmouth bass and panfish. While there is a scattering of submerged weeds near shore, look for deep cabbage down to 18 feet in front of the lodge on the west shore for the best results.

Area (5) The north bar is a well-known area for walleye and muskie. Adjacent drop-offs are fairly gradual and extend well-out into the lake. This bar has patches of submergent weeds and a sand/gravel bottom that walleye prefer. Cribs are present in 8 to 12 feet of water along the north shoreline.

FISHING TIPS - White Sand is a difficult lake to fish. It is important to use a depthfinder to effectively locate and work the available structure and drop-offs.

Clear water means that down-sized terminal tackle and light (4 to 6 pound) line are necessities for walleye anglers. Jig/minnow combinations are popular in spring and fall, while leeches and nightcrawlers are preferred summer baits.

The lake has a deserved reputation for producing trophy muskie. Big bucktails and jerkbaits are popular. Deep-diving crankbaits and weighted bucktails are recommended for the bar edges and steep shoreline breaks. Remember that low light conditions are a real plus, so fish early, late or on dark days.

CONCLUSION - White Sand Lake deserves your attention, but is a real challenge. There aren't many areas of typical structure such as, reefs, shoals and underwater islands. This tends to make your first outing on White Sand Lake difficult.

LAKE 23-12 (UNNAMED)
LAKE 26-2 (NELLIE LAKE)

LOCATION - In the east central part of the area, immediately north of White Sand Lake.

ACCESS

Type III (Lake 26-2): On the north side of the lake south of Concora Road; from Highway K, drive north on Nixon Lake Road for 1.4 miles. Proceed west on a Concora Road for 1.4 miles to the landing. There is a short carry-in with parking along the road.

Type III (Lake 23-12): On the southeast end of the lake, north of Concora Road; from Highway K, drive north on Nixon Lake Road for 1.4 miles. Proceed west for 1.6 miles to the landing. There is a 75- to 100-foot carry-in with parking along the road.

LAKE CHARACTERISTICS
Size and Depth - Lake 26-2; 12 acres and 15 feet.
Lake 23-12; 15 acres and 18 feet.

Water Source - Seepage lakes: No inlets or outlets.
Shoreline - 100% state-owned, mostly bog-lined.
Bottom - Sand and muck.
Water - Quite infertile.
Vegetation - Extremely limited.

FISHERY
SPECIES - Largemouth Bass, Perch, Bluegill, Pumpkinseed.
COMMENT - Small size and infertility limit the potential of both lakes.

LAKE MANAGEMENT
Lake Investigation Data - None.
Stocking - None recently.

CONCLUSION - These two potholes offer marginal fisheries. They are not worth your time if you are looking for anything but numbers of small panfish. Bass are found on the bog edges. Occasionally, a large fish can be found, even though neither lake possesses the water chemistry to maintain good numbers of nice-sized bass. The main asset of these lakes is the wilderness aesthetics.

NIXON LAKE

LOCATION - In the east central part of the area, north of Highway K and east of White Sand Lake.

ACCESS - Type V: Navigable access from Nixon Creek; the landing is on Nixon Lake Road 1.7 miles north of Highway K, (just north of the creek culvert pipe). It is a short, easy carry-in to the water, and parking is available north of the town landing on the other side of the road.

SPECIAL FEATURES - Only electric motors are allowed.

LAKE CHARACTERISTICS
Size and Depth - 110 acres and 5 feet.
Water Source - Drainage lake: An inlet on the southeast side from Partridge Creek and an outlet on the northwest side to Nixon Creek. Both are navigable.
Shoreline - 100% state-owned around the lake. The land adjacent to the creek on either side of the road is privately-owned. Most of the shore is lowland.
Bottom - Muck.
Water - Moderately fertile and quite murky.
Vegetation - Abundant weed cover exists throughout most of the lake; emergent, floating and submergent varieties are present.

FISHERY
SPECIES
Primary - Muskie, Perch, Bluegill.
Secondary - Largemouth Bass, Pumpkinseed.
Limited - Rock Bass, (Walleye).
COMMENT - Nixon Lake is rated as Class A muskie water, probably due to the excellent spawning habitat provided by submergent weeds.

LAKE MANAGEMENT
Lake Investigation Data - None.
Stocking - None recently.

FISHING TIPS - The key to fishing Nixon is to work the extensive weedbeds. Use brightly colored bucktails in these murky waters.

CONCLUSION - If you prefer an "off the beaten path" lake, Nixon is a good choice.

LOST CANOE LAKE

LOCATION - In the east central part of the area, adjacent to Highway K and east of Highway M.

ACCESS
Type III: On the north side of the lake; adjacent to Highway K about 2.5 miles east of Highway M by the lake sign. There is a roadside gravel parking area with a steep stairway approach down to a sand beach landing.

Type III: On the north side of the lake; adjacent to Highway K about 2.7 miles east of Highway M. There is a roadside gravel parking area and steep approach to a sand beach landing.

RELATED SERVICES
Boat Rentals - Yes.
Resorts - None.
Campgrounds - None, except for a wilderness site on the large state-owned island.
Public Park - There is a picnic table at the east access on Highway K.

LAKE CHARACTERISTICS
Size and Depth - 249 acres and 44 feet.
Water Source - Seepage lake: A minor inlet on the southeast end from Escanaba lake and no outlet.

Shoreline - 85% state-owned.

Bottom - Mostly sand with rock and some muck.

Water - Fairly fertile and quite clear.

Vegetation - Moderate densities of emergent, submergent and floating varieties are present, except on most of the south shoreline.

FISHERY
SPECIES

Primary - Largemouth Bass, Northern Pike, Perch, Rock Bass, Bluegill.

Secondary - Smallmouth Bass, Pumpkinseed, Crappie.

Limited - Walleye, Muskie.

COMMENT - Largemouth bass and northern pike are the dominant gamefish.

LAKE MANAGEMENT

Lake Investigation Data - None.

Stocking - None recently.

Treatment - Thirty-two log fish shelters were installed in 1968.

FISHING TIPS - Those who take the time to launch a small boat on this lake find that weedbeds, shoreline downed timber and the island with an adjacent sand/gravel bar are important fishing locations.

The shallow east half of the lake has weeds, cribs and submerged wood. Much of the southwest corner has good weed cover and should be worked for northern, bass and panfish.

Weed patches in the middle of the lake offer decent northern and muskie habitat. Try just west of the large center island and in the northwest corner.

Pay attention to the island area, being sure not to overlook the area of weeds and cribs just southeast of the island.

CONCLUSION - The lack of a decent access limits pressure on this lake. Lost Canoe holds a varied community of gamefish, including bass, northern and an occasional muskie. The best action is for bass, northern and panfish.

STEVENSON SPRINGS
(STEVENSON CREEK FLOWAGE)

LOCATION - In the east central part of the section, east of Highway M and south of Highway K.

ACCESS - Type III: On the west end of the springs at the earthen dam; turn east off Highway M at Nebish Road. This intersection is marked by the large "Fishery Research Area" sign. Drive east for 0.8 mile to a snowmobile trail. Turn north and continue for 1.4 miles to the springs and creek. This is a good trail for any vehicle. A beach landing and parking area are present.

LAKE CHARACTERISTICS
Size and Depth - 25 acres and 10 feet.
Water Source - Springs: The flowage is formed by a complex of spring ponds. The Stevenson Creek outlet flows into Trout Lake.
Shoreline - 100% state-owned.
Bottom - Mostly muck.
Water - Quite fertile and clear.
Vegetation - Emergent and submergent weeds are present.

FISHERY
SPECIES - Brook Trout, Perch.

LAKE MANAGEMENT
Lake Investigation Data - Recent test nettings to evaluate the brook trout population have found more trout in the area just east of Highway M than near the spring. A good number of these were 6 inches or larger.

Stocking

STEVENSON SPRINGS STOCKING SUMMARY			
YEAR	SPECIES	NUMBER	SIZE
1988	Brook Trout	500	6"
1989	Brook Trout	500	6"
1990	Brook Trout	500	6"

CONCLUSION - This 25-acre flowage remains "off the beaten path" so as to not attract a crowd of trout fishermen.

PALLETTE LAKE

LOCATION - In the east central part of the area; south of Highway K, east of Highway M, and immediately west of Escanaba Lake.

ACCESS

A **Type IV:** To the south end of the lake; from Highway M, take Nebish Road east for 3.1 miles to the lake sign. A parking area and walk-in access are found.

B **Type IV:** On the east side of the lake, a canoe portage from Escanaba Lake.

PALLETTE LAKE

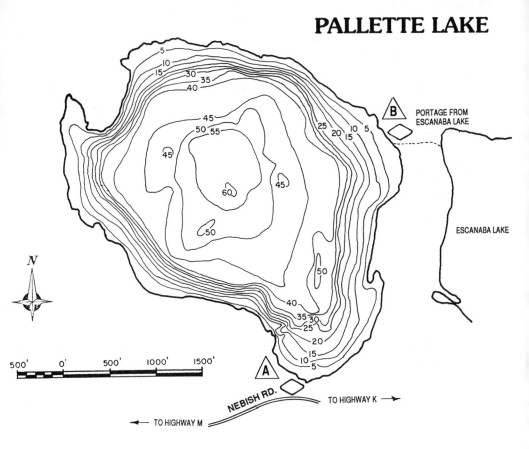

RELATED SERVICES

Campgrounds - Yes, wilderness sites are available.
Resorts - None.
Boat Rental - None.

SPECIAL FEATURES - As part of the Northern Highland Research Area (formerly called Five Lakes Research Project), Pallette Lake is currently managed for smallmouth bass. Special regulations apply. In 1987, lake trout were closed to angling.

LAKE CHARACTERISTICS

Size and Depth - 173 acres and 65 feet.
Water Source - Seepage lake: No inlet or outlet.
Shoreline - 100% state-owned.
Bottom - Mostly gravel and rock with some sand.
Water - Infertile and very clear.
Vegetation - Extremely limited and confined to a narrow shoreline area.

FISHERY
SPECIES
Primary - Smallmouth Bass, Northern Pike, Cisco.
Secondary - Perch, Rock Bass.
Limited - Lake Trout.

COMMENT - The Trout Lake strain of lake trout have been introduced and are protected by a closed season. Northern pike and smallmouth bass are low in density, but high quality fish are present. Currently, studies are focusing on developing trophy smallmouth bass.

LAKE MANAGEMENT
Lake Investigation Data - Studies are conducted periodically to evaluate the fishery.
Stocking - None recently.

CONCLUSION - Pallette Lake can provide action for above average smallmouth bass and northern pike.

ESCANABA LAKE

LOCATION - In the east central part of the book area, south of Highway K and east of Highway M.

ACCESS - Type I (Public): On the south side of the lake; from Highway M (at the "Fishery Research Area" sign), turn east on Nebish Road for 3.8 miles. Turn left on the marked road to the landing. A concrete ramp and loading pier are provided. The paved parking area is located at the cross country ski trail entrance.

RELATED SERVICES
Boat Rentals - Yes.
Resorts - None.
Campgrounds - Yes, two wilderness sites.

SPECIAL FEATURES - Escanaba is the most famous lake of the Northern Highland Research Area. Special fishing rules apply and all anglers must check-in with the research office adjacent to the landing before and after fishing.

LAKE CHARACTERISTICS
Size and Depth - 288 acres and 25 feet.
Water Source - Drainage lake: A small inlet on the east side from Mystery Lake and a small outlet on the north end.
Shoreline - 100% state-owned. Wetlands border the east side.
Bottom - Sand, gravel and rock with minor areas of muck.
Water - Moderately fertile and fairly clear.

Vegetation - Moderate amounts of emergent, submergent and floating varieties along the shoreline.

FISHERY
SPECIES
Primary - Walleye, Muskie, Perch.
Secondary - Northern Pike, Rock Bass, Pumpkinseed.
Limited - Largemouth Bass, Smallmouth Bass, Bluegill.
COMMENT - Walleye are clearly the most abundant and most sought after species. The majority of fish taken are between 10 and 12 inches. However, a fair number of larger fish are present. Muskie numbers have remained stable with many fish in the 30- to 36-inch range. Every year a few fish in the 30-pound range are taken.

Perch provide consistent action year-round. The size structure has remained stable, with most fish averaging 7- to 10-inches. Some perch in the 11-inch range are present.

LAKE MANAGEMENT
Lake Investigation Data - As the "home" lake of the research area, Escanaba Lake has been the focus of many pioneering research projects.

The results of many of these studies are used to help formulate fishing regulations and management strategies for lakes throughout the state. The information compiled from the mandatory creel census and the various netting and electrofishing surveys represents one of the most comprehensive collections of fisheries data available to biologists anywhere. Important projects have included:

● Growth studies on northern pike and muskie.
● Angler harvest of sizes and age groups of walleye over a 24-year period.
● Factors that influence the success of walleye natural reproduction.
● The impact of state walleye spawning activities (egg-taking) on the natural reproduction of walleye.
● What determines when walleye bite.
● Length limit studies on northern pike.

Originally, projects on Escanaba Lake focused on the relationship between bag limits and/or seasons and their effects on walleye populations. Part of the findings show that annual natural mortality of adult walleye is about 15 percent. Fishing mortality adds another 25% per year. The results of the continuing creel census are summarized in the chart on the top of page 96.

ESCANABA LAKE

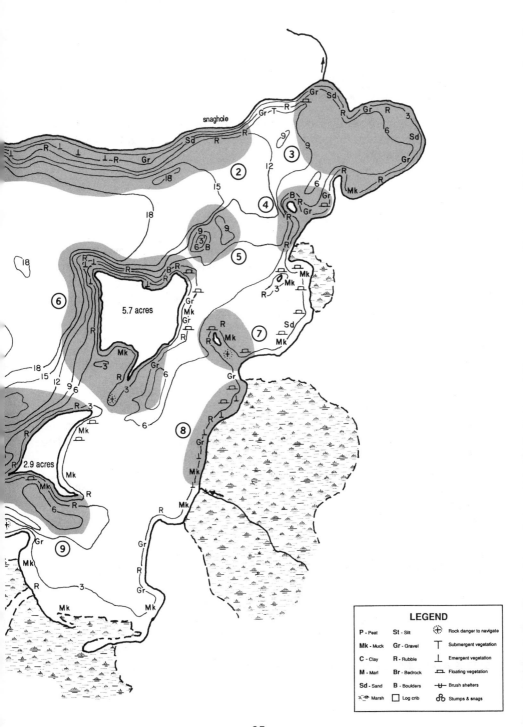

ESCANABA LAKE CREEL CENSUS			
SPECIES	1988	1989	1990*
Walleye	3,906	4,278	2,453
Northern Pike	19	36	21
Muskie	25	44	38
Perch	3,082	2,189	2,676
Rock Bass	15	18	5
Smallmouth Bass	0	1	0

* Does not include the ice fishing season

The survey clearly shows the popularity of walleye, perch and muskie. Fishing pressure for perch was heaviest in early spring and during the ice fishing season.

Stocking - None recently.

LAKE SURVEY MAP - Fishing Areas Shaded

Area (1) The 12- to 18-foot depths off the northwest bay can provide excellent action for spring walleye. Work jig/minnow combos along the gravel bottom.

Area (2) This long stretch of gravel shoreline yields walleye and perch. Depths down to 18 feet are prime; concentrate on the scattered cabbage beds and steeper breaks. On the northeast end of the area, a 15-foot breakline is locally known as the "Snaghole." This spot can produce good early season walleye fishing.

Area (3) Work the shoreline wood and available cover in this northern bay for pike and largemouth bass.

Area (4) Cast in-line spinners around this small island for muskie. Pay attention to the primary and secondary drop-offs.

Area (5) North of the large island is a shallow bar and 10-foot flat that is well-known for muskie.

Area (6) The rock and gravel drop-offs around the large island yield walleye and muskie. Use a depthfinder locate the inside and outside turns of the breakline. The shallow bars south of the island are favorites for muskie and walleye.

Area (7) Muskie are found in the shallow water around this small island.

Area (8) Cast the shallow shoreline cover along this section of east shoreline for panfish and northern pike.

Area (9) This small island has a variety of structure that attracts walleye, muskie and northern pike. A depthfinder is valuable in working the subtle changes in depth or bottom content.

Area (10) Walleye frequent this long gravel point. Backtroll live bait rigs along the primary breaks.

Area (11) Vertical jig the perimeter of this rock bar for walleye. This small structure is located approximately 1,000 feet from the mouth of the boat landing bay.

Area (12) Walleye, muskie and northern pike are taken from the steep shoreline breaks along the south shore. Cast parallel to these breaks to be effective.

FISHING TIPS - Escanaba Lake produces its best walleye action during low light periods. Use a fluorescent red jig, or a #6 hook and split shot, tipped with a minnow early in the season. By June, leeches generally are more productive. Slip-bobbers are effective for working the shallow shoreline cover and rock bars.

Look for muskie along the scattered weedbeds and the shoreline breaks. Black, purple and yellow bucktails are preferred during most of the year. Deep-running crankbaits are effective when working the deeper structure.

CONCLUSION - Escanaba Lake is surprisingly productive and offers a variety of fishing. The combination of good numbers of fish and challenging structure attracts many anglers.

NEBISH LAKE

LOCATION - In the east central part of the area, east of Highway M, and south of Highway K and Escanaba Lake.

ACCESS - Type I (Public): On the west end of the lake; from Highway M, drive east on Nebish Road for 3.3 miles to the marked access road. Turn south for 0.2 mile to the landing. A shallow, unimproved sand ramp, loading pier and parking area are present.

RELATED SERVICES
    Boat Rentals - Yes.
    Resorts - None.
    Campground - Yes, two wilderness sites.

SPECIAL FEATURES - As part of the Northern Highland Research Area. Specific fishing rules are in effect. All anglers must check-in at the research station in Escanaba Lake before and after fishing.

LAKE CHARACTERISTICS
    Size and Depth - 95 acres and 50 feet.
    Water Source - Seepage lake: No inlet or outlet.
    Shoreline - 100% state-owned.
    Bottom - Gravel and rock with some muck.
    Water - Slightly fertile and very clear. Oxygen levels are adequate to 30 feet.
    Vegetation - Extremely limited and confined to a narrow shoreline zone.

FISHERY
    SPECIES - Smallmouth Bass, Perch.
    COMMENT - Smallmouth bass are abundant and are the only predator species found in the lake. A very good density of fast-growing fish are

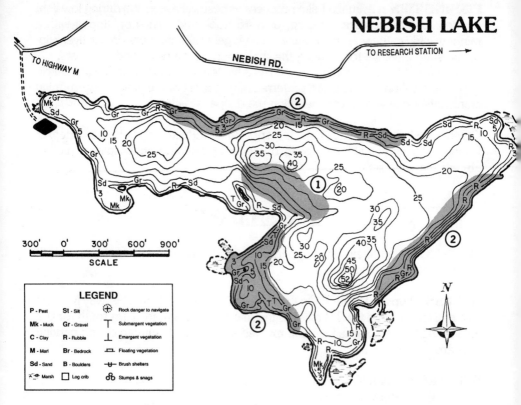

NEBISH LAKE

present. Due to angling pressure, however, trophy fish are limited. The perch population is dominated by small fish.

LAKE MANAGEMENT
Lake Investigation Data - Periodic surveys are used to assess the status of the fishery.
Stocking - None recently.

LAKE SURVEY MAP - Fishing Areas Shaded
Area (1) The 10- to 20-foot depths east of the island yield both perch and smallmouth bass.
Area (2) Much of the steep shoreline has a gravel/rock bottom and downed timber that attract smallmouth bass. Work light jigs tipped with nightcrawlers or leeches tight to the shoreline cover. Small floating Rapalas or Mepps Aglia spinners can also be effective.

FISHING TIPS - Work the rocky drop-offs and submerged timber with small crayfish-colored crankbaits. Live bait rigs tipped with nightcrawlers, leeches or minnows are always good selections. Try twitching Rapalas along the edges of the submerged timber.

CONCLUSION - Nebish Lake has a hard rock bottom, light amounts of vegetation and limited potential to support large fish. It offers fun fishing as numerous 8- to 11-inch smallmouth are available. Expect quantity, not quality.

MYSTERY LAKE

LOCATION - In the east central part of the book area, south of Highway K and east of Escanaba Lake.

ACCESS - Type III: On the south end of the lake; from Highway M take Nebish Road east for 4.5 miles to the marked access road. Follow the signs 0.1 mile to the parking area. The landing is reached by a short easy carry-in through an opening in the bog. There is limited parking.

SPECIAL FEATURES - Part of the Northern Highland Fishery Research Area. Special fishing regulations are in effect and anglers are required to check in at the research station before and after fishing.

LAKE CHARACTERISTICS
> **Size and Depth** - 20 acres and 6 feet.
> **Water Source** - Drained lake: An outlet on the west end to Escanaba Lake.
> **Shoreline** - 100% state-owned. Mostly bog lined.
> **Bottom** - Mostly muck.
> **Water** - Moderately infertile and a little murky. Winterkill due to oxygen depletion is common.
> **Vegetation** - Scarce.

FISHERY
> **SPECIES** - Northern Pike, Largemouth Bass, Perch.
> **COMMENT** - Winterkill normally limits the fishery to a few perch.

LAKE MANAGEMENT
> **Lake Investigation Data** - None.
> **Stocking** - None recently.

CONCLUSION - Mystery Lake serves as a research lake for the study of fish species and changing fish communities in winterkill lakes. It is extremely limited in angling value.

SPRUCE LAKE

LOCATION - In the east central part of the area, south of Highway K and east of Nebish and Escanaba lakes.

ACCESS - Type III: On the north side of the lake; from Highway M, drive east 4.5 miles to the landing on the south side of the road slightly west of the Mystery Lake access. There is a short, steep grade down to the lake, and roadside parking is available.

SPECIAL FEATURES - Part of the Northern Highland Research Area. Special fishing regulations apply.

LAKE CHARACTERISTICS

Size and Depth - 16 acres and 11 feet.
Water Source - Seepage lake: No inlet or outlet.
Shoreline - 100% state-owned.
Bottom - Primarily sand with some gravel and a little muck.
Water - Quite infertile and reasonable clear.
Vegetation - Entirely rimmed by bog.

FISHERY

SPECIES - Largemouth Bass, Perch.
COMMENT - The lake has a good population of largemouth bass from 12 to 15 inches. Each year a few 5-pound fish are caught.

LAKE MANAGEMENT

Lake Investigation Data - Over the years, studies have been conducted on Spruce Lake to evaluate the impact of various size and season limits.
Stocking - Largemouth Bass were last stocked in the early 1980's.

CONCLUSION - Spruce Lake is a typical bog lake with extremely low fertility. The bass fishery provides decent action, and fishing pressure is generally light due to the carry-in access.

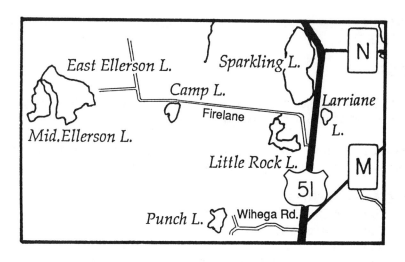

Mid Ellerson Lake

East Ellerson Lake

Camp Lake

Sparkling Lake (Silver L.)

Little Rock Lake

Larraine Lake

Punch Lake (Boyle L.)

MID ELLERSON LAKE

LOCATION - In the southwest part of the area, west of Highway 51 and south of the Trout River.

ACCESS

Type IV: On the east side of the lake, a portage from East Ellerson Lake is possible over the adjoining state land. (See East Ellerson Lake).

Type IV: On the south end of the lake, via a ½-mile carry-in over state and paper company land, from the curve in the "East Boundary Trail" road.

LAKE CHARACTERISTICS
    Size and Depth - 60 acres and 51 feet.
    Water Source - Seepage lake: No inlet or outlet.
    Shoreline - 35% state-owned, only on the east side.
    Bottom - Mostly sand with small quantities of gravel and muck.
    Water - Very infertile and clear.
    Vegetation - Confined to a narrow shoreline fringe, primarily emergent and floating varieties.

FISHERY
    SPECIES
        Primary - Largemouth Bass, Bluegill, Rock Bass, Perch.
        Secondary - Pumpkinseed.
        Limited - Muskie, Smallmouth Bass.
    COMMENT - Largemouth bass are the dominant gamefish. Panfish, especially bluegill and rock bass, appear to be stunted. Mid Ellerson Lake is Class C muskie water.

LAKE MANAGEMENT
    Lake Investigation Data - None recently.
    Stocking - None.

FISHING TIPS - Much of the same habitat exists as in East Ellerson, but there are deeper shoreline drop-offs on Mid. Try working the shoreline weed and wood cover for bass.

CONCLUSION - Except for the occasional decent bass or muskie, there is little to attract anglers. The dramatic infertility of Mid Ellerson is a hindrance to a respectable fishery.

EAST ELLERSON LAKE

LOCATION - In the southwest portion of the area, west of Highway 51 and south of the Trout River.

ACCESS - Type IV: On the east side of the lake; there is an access road (fire lane) off Highway 51 at the "Little Rock Lake" sign, about 1 mile north of the Highway M intersection. Follow this dirt road in a westerly direction past Little Rock and Camp Lakes a total of 2.5 miles to a fork. Stay to the right for another 0.3 mile. The barricaded dirt road to the west is closed to motorized vehicles. Continue west on foot for 0.7 mile to the lake.

LAKE CHARACTERISTICS
Size and Depth - 136 acres and 26 feet.
Water Source - Seepage lake: No inlet or outlet.
Shoreline - 100% state-owned. Primarily upland.
Bottom - Mostly sand with small amounts of muck and gravel.
Water - Moderately infertile and fairly clear.
Vegetation - Wild rice, bulrush, lily pad and cabbage are present in moderate amounts.

FISHERY
SPECIES
Primary - Largemouth Bass, Bluegill, Perch, Rock Bass.
Secondary - Smallmouth Bass.
Limited - Muskie, Walleye, Northern Pike.
COMMENT - The state rates East Ellerson Lake as Class A muskie water, although little is known of the population status. Largemouth bass are the most abundant predator and have maintained their numbers through natural reproduction. A small population of walleye, muskie and northern pike are believed to exist.

LAKE MANAGEMENT
Lake Investigation Data - None.
Stocking - None recently.

FISHING TIPS - Vegetation and submerged wood are important factors in fishing East Ellerson. The bay to the left of the access is lined with weeds and offers early season bass fishing. The west shoreline has good depths plus lily pads and submerged shoreline brush that yield bass. Try the sandy bottom area along the north shoreline for an occasional smallmouth bass. A cabbage bed just southwest of the access should be cast for muskie.

CONCLUSION - East Ellerson is a medium-sized wilderness lake that offers the thrill of discovery. The lake sustains a decent bass population that will remain as long as fishermen are willing to practice catch-and-release.

CAMP LAKE

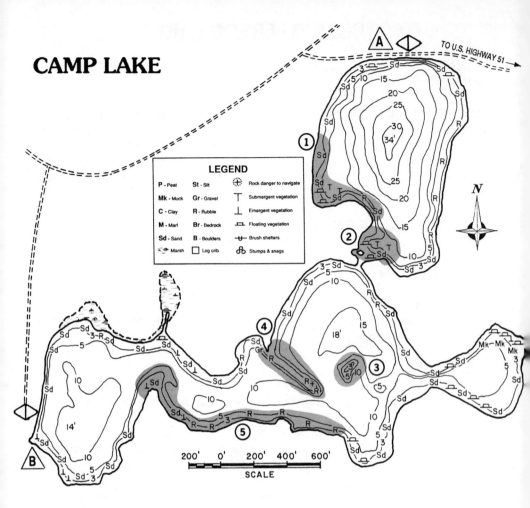

LEGEND

P - Peat	**St** - Silt	⊕ Rock danger to navigate
Mk - Muck	**Gr** - Gravel	T Submergent vegetation
C - Clay	**R** - Rubble	⊥ Emergent vegetation
M - Marl	**Br** - Bedrock	⌐⌐ Floating vegetation
Sd - Sand	**B** - Boulders	∪ Brush shelters
Marsh	☐ Log crib	⬡⬡ Stumps & snags

200' 0' 200' 400' 600'
SCALE

CAMP LAKE

LOCATION - In the southwest part of the area, west of Highway 51.

ACCESS

△**A** **Type III:** On the north side of the lake; there is an access road (fire lane) off Highway 51 at the "Little Rock Lake" sign one mile north of the Highway M intersection. Follow this dirt road past the east and north ends of Little Rock Lake (west off "51", then north, then west again) for a total of 2.1 miles to a short easy carry-in on the left. There is an opening for parking.

△**B** **Type III:** On the west end of the lake; take the above fire lane west past the above landing to the second fork. Turn left to the landing area.

SPECIAL FEATURES - The two basins are connected by a channel that is navigable during average water levels. There is a consumption advisory on bass.

LAKE CHARACTERISTICS
Size and Depth - 37 acres and 19 feet.
Water Source - Seepage lake: No inlet or outlet.
Shoreline - 100% state-owned. Mainly upland.
Bottom - 75% sand, 20% muck, 5% gravel.
Water - Very infertile and quite clear. Oxygen levels are good.
Vegetation - Moderate weed cover is available, typically lily pads and bulrush.

FISHERY
SPECIES - Largemouth Bass, Muskie, Bluegill, Perch, Pumpkinseed, (Smallmouth Bass).
COMMENT - The fishery is dominated by an over-abundant bluegill population. Perch are also numerous but tend to be of small average size. Largemouth bass are self-sustaining.

LAKE MANAGEMENT
Lake Investigation Data - None recently.
Stocking - None.

LAKE SURVEY MAP - Fishing Areas Shaded
Area (1) Work the weedline of the small bay and the sharp drop-off for bass, bluegill and the occasional muskie.
Area (2) Look to the deeper weed edges in the channel for bass, especially in the 4- to 10-foot zone.
Area (3) This shallow 3-foot sunken island attracts bass and bluegill. Fish the deeper edges for better-sized bluegill, and a possible bonus muskie.
Area (4) Work the 3- to 10-foot depths along this submerged rock bar for bass and bluegill.
Area (5) Much of the south shoreline offers weeds and a steep drop-off to 10 feet that attract largemouth and bluegill. The shoreline point on the west side of this area should be cast for muskie.

FISHING TIPS - Emergent and floating vegetation are key fish-holding areas on Camp Lake. Always try the deeper weed edges for larger bluegill, though they are rare in this water.

CONCLUSION - Camp Lake is a fine wilderness lake. Its isolated location means that fishing pressure is very light. Bass and bluegill provide most of the action. A few large bass are possible, but bluegill over 8 inches are rare.

SPARKLING LAKE (SILVER LAKE)

LOCATION - In the south central part of the area, west of, and adjacent to Highway 51 at the Highway N intersection.

ACCESS - Type I (Public): On the east side of the lake near the north end; this unmarked, unimproved access is adjacent to Highway 51, just north of the Highway N/51 intersection. There is limited parking and a gravel/sand ramp.

RELATED SERVICES
Public Parks - A wayside on Highway 51 just south of the Highway N intersection. No landing is available, but drinking water and restrooms are provided.

LAKE CHARACTERISTICS
Size and Depth - 127 acres and 64 feet.
Water Source - Seepage lake: No inlet or outlet.
Shoreline - 86% state-owned, all except the northwest side.
Bottom - Mostly sand with gravel and rock.
Water - Quite infertile and exceptionally clear.
Vegetation - Limited; confined to a very narrow shoreline zone, especially on the south end.

FISHERY
SPECIES
    Primary - Walleye, Perch, Rock Bass, Sucker, Smelt.
    Secondary - Muskie, Brown Trout, Cisco.
    Limited - Smallmouth Bass, Largemouth Bass, (Bluegill), (Pumpkinseed).
COMMENT - The state rates Sparkling Lake as Class A muskie water, but muskie are not very abundant. Walleye are present and seem to be reproducing naturally. Brown trout were introduced in 1989 in an attempt to establish a two-story fishery.

LAKE MANAGEMENT
Lake Investigation Data - None recently.
Stocking

SPARKLING LAKE STOCKING SUMMARY			
YEAR	SPECIES	NUMBER	SIZE
1989	Brown Trout	3,000	Fry
	Brown Trout	2,000	Yearling
1990	Brown Trout	4,500	Yearling

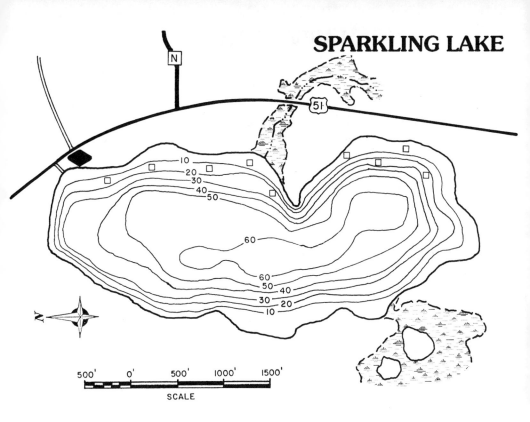

Treatment - Twenty log cribs were installed in the late 1950's. Despite their deteriorated condition, they are a factor in fishing success.

FISHING TIPS - Most walleye are caught along the east shore, near the cribs that are adjacent to the wayside. Also check the cribs along the north shoreline in front of the cottages and homes. Try the south end or any shoreline wood for muskie.

The available cover in the narrow shoreline zone and adjacent deep water tends to hold the most fish. Panfish are often caught near the remains of the old cribs.

CONCLUSION - Sparkling Lake is beautiful water to be on, but a number of factors make fishing difficult: vegetation is scarce, the water is very clear, and the bottom lacks distinct structure.

LITTLE ROCK LAKE

LOCATION - In the southwest part of the area, immediately west of Highway 51.

NOTE: Little Rock Lake has been completely closed to public access since 1984. A joint DNR, University of Wisconsin, and Environmental Protection Agency 10-year experiment on acidification is being conducted on this lake.

LARRAINE LAKE

LOCATION - In the south central part of the area, just east of Highway 51 and south of Highway N.

ACCESS - Type III: On the west side of the lake; this site is adjacent to Highway 51, about 1¼ miles north of the Highway M intersection. There is a sign on the road and parking is available along the highway shoulder.

LAKE CHARACTERISTICS
    Size and Depth - 10 acres and 6 feet.
    Water Source - Seepage lake: No inlet or outlet.
    Shoreline - 100% state-owned.
    Bottom - Muck.
    Water - Extremely infertile and moderately clear.
    Vegetation - Virtually none; much of the shoreline is rimmed with bog.

FISHERY
    SPECIES - Largemouth Bass, Bluegill, Perch, Pumpkinseed.
    COMMENT - This fishery is characterized by slow growth and is dominated by small panfish and bass.

LAKE MANAGEMENT
    Lake Investigation Data - None recently.
    Stocking - None.

CONCLUSION - The infertility of this roadside pothole limits the fishery. Decent numbers of small bass are available for those who want to launch a canoe. However, quality fish are uncommon.

PUNCH LAKE (BOYLE LAKE)

LOCATION - In the southwest part of the area, west of Highway 51 at the Highway M intersection.

ACCESS - Type IV: On the northeast side of the lake; take Wihega Road west off Highway 51 for 0.8 mile to a state logging road entrance just before the sharp left curve. Take this fairly rough road for ¼ mile to a gate. Access is about 350 feet from this point through the woods.

LAKE CHARACTERISTICS
    Size and Depth - 21 acres and 40 feet.
    Water Source - Seepage lake: No inlet or outlet.
    Shoreline - 90% state-owned, except for the south end.

Bottom - 60% sand, 40% muck.
Vegetation - Limited to a narrow shoreline fringe.

FISHERY
SPECIES - Largemouth Bass, Bluegill, Perch, Pumpkinseed.
COMMENT - Bluegill are stunted and extremely abundant.

LAKE MANAGEMENT
Lake Investigation Data - None recently.
Stocking - None recently.

CONCLUSION - There is little available in Punch Lake to warrant your attention, other than small bluegill and perch. Fishing time is better spent elsewhere.

SECTION 7

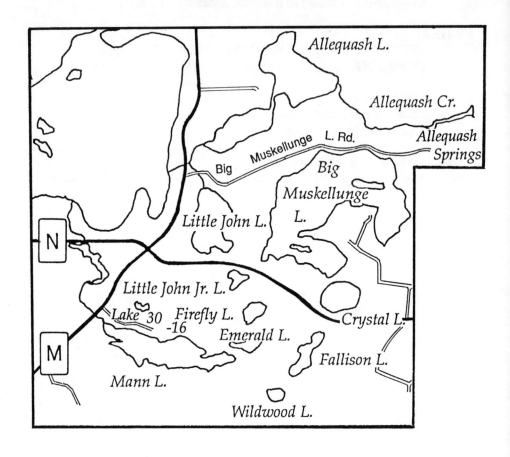

ALLEQUASH LAKE

LOCATION - In the southeast part of the area, north of Highway N and just east of Highway M.

ACCESS - Type I (Public): On the west side of the narrows connecting the two basins; from Highway M, take the paved access road east for about 1 mile to the landing. The marked access road is 2.3 miles north of the Highway M/N intersection. There is a concrete slab ramp, turn-around, parking area and loading pier.

RELATED SERVICES
> **Boat Rentals** - None.
> **Resorts** - None.
> **Campgrounds** - Four state wilderness campsites.

SPECIAL FEATURES - The state has instituted an experimental 40-inch minimum size limit on muskie. Only electric motors are allowed on the south lake to protect the wild rice.

LAKE CHARACTERISTICS
> **Size and Depth** - 426 acres and 24 feet.
> **Water Source** - Drainage lake: A shallow inlet (Allequash Creek) on the east side from Allequash Springs, and a navigable outlet (Allequash Creek) on the west end to Trout Lake.
> **Shoreline** - 100% state-owned.
> **Bottom** - 50% muck, 25% sand, 20% gravel, 5% rock and boulder. The entire south lake and the west side of the north lake are predominantly muck.
> **Water** - Quite fertile and moderately clear.
> **Vegetation** - Submergent and emergent vegetation are abundant. Milfoil, wild rice, coontail, large leaf cabbage, narrow leaf cabbage, bulrush and lily pads are the primary species.

FISHERY
> **SPECIES**
>> **Primary** - Muskie, Northern Pike, Largemouth Bass, Bluegill, Rock Bass.
>> **Secondary** - Walleye, Crappie, Pumpkinseed, Perch.
>> **Limited** - Smallmouth Bass.
>
> **COMMENT** - Walleye are stocked because of limited natural reproduction. Largemouth bass reproduce naturally and are present in good numbers. Bluegill are the most common panfish and display good growth rates and average sizes. Crappie and bluegill are the main panfish species pursued by anglers. Northern pike are numerous and compete with the muskie.

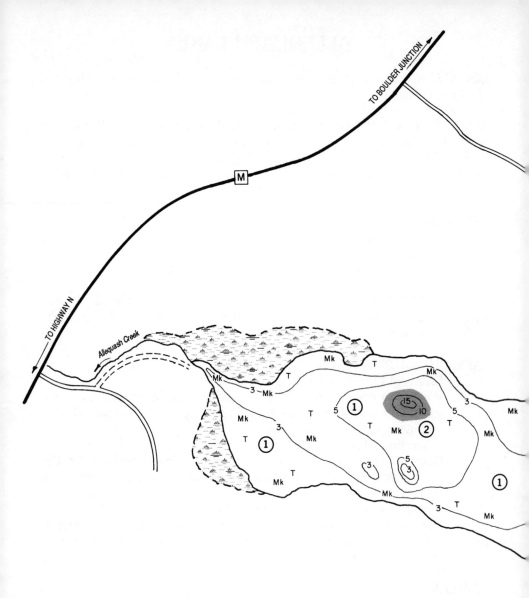

TO BOULDER JUNCTION

TO HIGHWAY N

Allequash Creek

M

LEGEND

P - Peat	St - Silt	⊕ Rock danger to navigate
Mk - Muck	Gr - Gravel	⊤ Submergent vegetation
C - Clay	R - Rubble	⊥ Emergent vegetation
M - Marl	Br - Bedrock	▱ Floating vegetation
Sd - Sand	B - Boulders	⨆ Brush shelters
⚶ Marsh	☐ Log crib	⚭ Stumps & snags

ALLEQUASH LAKE

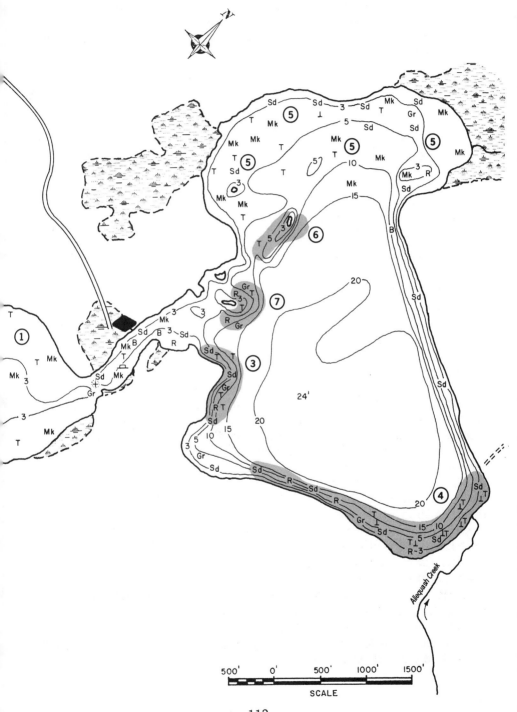

SCALE
500'   0'   500'   1000'   1500'

LAKE MANAGEMENT

Lake Investigation Data - An electrofishing survey was conducted to assess walleye natural reproduction. No walleye young-of-the-year were seen but good numbers of largemouth bass were captured. Of interest, researchers confirmed that large numbers of 6- to 10-inch bluegill were present. The study recommended that walleye should be stocked on an alternate year basis.

Stocking

ALLEQUASH LAKE STOCKING SUMMARY			
YEAR	SPECIES	NUMBER	SIZE
1983	Walleye	20,000	3"
	Muskie	250	Fingerling
1986	Walleye	51,300	Fry
1987	Muskie	900	8"
	Walleye	20,000	3"
1988	Muskie	27,000	Fry
1989	Walleye	31,060	Fingerling
	Muskie	67,500	Fry
	Muskie	400	Fingerling
1990	Muskie	103,950	Fry

Treatment - None recently.

LAKE SURVEY MAP - Fishing Areas Shaded

Area (1) The vast majority of the south lake is laced with cabbage and wild rice. Use lure and bait presentations that work effectively in weeds. Concentrate on the weed points and inside turns of the weedline. During summer, the deeper weeds provide the most consistent action. Muskie, northern pike, largemouth bass and panfish are available. Early season largemouth bass relate close to the shoreline, especially during the pre-spawn and spawn periods. In spring, crappie are taken on slip bobbers rigs along the edges of the rice beds.

Area (2) Use a jig/live bait combo or a slip bobber presentation to take walleye from this 15-foot hole.

Area (3) This shoreline point east of the narrows has a gravel bottom and scattered submergent weeds that attract muskie and walleye. Use a depthfinder to effectively work the 5- to 15-foot depths around the point.

Area (4) In early spring, walleye and muskie use the hard bottom along the southeast shoreline. The northeast bay is lined with reeds, and the adjacent deep cabbage holds bluegill and an occasional muskie.

Area (5) The broad, relatively shallow weed flat at the north end of the lake yields northern pike, muskie and walleye. As a general rule, work the weedlines found at the 4- to 8-foot depths.

Area (6) A fairly sharp drop-off south of the island is a popular walleye spot. The sharpest break is located on east side of the island from 8 to 18 feet.

Area (7) A shallow underwater point east of the island contains gravel, rocks and weeds. Use a depthfinder to locate the changes in bottom types and the exact shape of the bar. Cast deep-diving crankbaits along the edges of this structure for muskie and walleye.

FISHING TIPS - Weeds are important to fishing success on Allequash Lake. Jig/minnow combinations give way to leeches by June as the preferred walleye bait. Spinnerbaits and "twitched" balsa minnow lures take bass from the shallow weed cover. Texas-rigged plastic worms are effective in the heavy cover of the south lake.

Muskie anglers prefer yellow or chartreuse lures on bright days and orange or black baits on dark days. Dark-colored jerkbaits and live suckers are suggested late in the season.

CONCLUSION - Allequash clearly ranks as one of the top lakes in the area. While not known as a trophy fishery for muskie or walleye, the good numbers of decent-sized fish attract knowledgeable anglers. Expect moderate to heavy fishing pressure on this productive lake.

ALLEQUASH SPRINGS

LOCATION - In the southeast part of the area, east of Highway M and Allequash Lake, and north of Highway N and Big Muskellunge Lake.

ACCESS

Type III: On the northeast end of the springs; from Highway M, take Big Muskellunge Lake Road east for 3.8 miles to an unmarked road on the north side. Proceed north for 1.0 mile to an unmarked dirt road on the left. Follow this road for 0.2 mile to a fork, and stay to the left for another 0.3 mile to the springs. There is a short easy carry-in landing. This access road is rough but passable for most cars.

Type V: Navigable access via Allequash Creek from Allequash Lake.

SPECIAL FEATURES - Electric motors only.

LAKE CHARACTERISTICS
    Size and Depth - 12 acres and 5 feet.
    Water Source - Spring-fed ponds: An outlet on the west end to Allequash Lake.
    Shoreline - 100% state-owned. Difficult access to most of the shore.
    Bottom - 50% sand, 40% muck, 10% gravel.
    Water - Moderately infertile and light brown in color.
    Vegetation - Limited.

FISHERY

SPECIES - Brook Trout, Perch, Pumpkinseed.

COMMENT - Allequash Springs and Allequash Creek are managed by the state for brook trout. It consists of four spring ponds. The largest is at the source on the east end and is 10 acres. The other three are ½ mile downstream and total a little more than two acres.

LAKE MANAGEMENT

Lake Investigation Data - In a recent survey, the largest brook trout sampled was 8 inches. Of the 149 trout taken, 25 percent were 6 inches or larger. A later fall sampling produced 16 trout, of which one was 18½ inches.

Stocking - About 500 brook trout are stocked every year.

CONCLUSION - For the avid trout fisherman, Allequash Springs offers a pleasant wilderness outing and a chance at catchable brook trout. A canoe is recommended.

BIG MUSKELLUNGE LAKE

LOCATION - In the southeast part of the area, just north of Highway N and east of Highway M.

ACCESS

A **Type I (Public):** In the southwest corner of the lake in West Bay; from Highway N, take the marked access road north 0.2 miles to the landing. A paved parking area, concrete ramp, restrooms and loading pier are provided.

B **Type I (Public):** On the southeast end of the lake in South Bay; this landing is part of the state campground adjacent to both Crystal and Big Muskellunge Lakes. Take the well-marked access road north of Highway N to the landing.

C **Type III (Public):** On the north side of the lake; from Highway M, take Big Muskellunge Lake Road east for 2.3 miles to several roadside clearings with small unimproved parking areas. The one furthest east is marked and has a good gravel beach.

RELATED SERVICES

Boat Rentals - Yes.
Resorts - None.
Campgrounds - Yes, on the southeast end and a group campsite on the northeast end.
Public Parks - Yes.

LAKE CHARACTERISTICS

Size and Depth - 930 acres and 70 feet.

Water Source - Seepage lake: No inlet and one intermittent outlet.

Shoreline - 70% state-owned and mostly upland.

Bottom - 50% sand, 26% gravel, 20% muck, 4% rubble.

Water - Moderately fertile and fairly clear. Dissolved oxygen is adequate at lower depths.

Vegetation - Abundant, with cabbage, bulrush and water lily the most common. Cabbage is primarily confined to the South Bay and West Bay. There is scattered weed cover along the west and north shore, around Deer Island, and at the south end of Pearses Bay.

FISHERY

SPECIES

Primary - Walleye, Muskie, Bluegill, Pumpkinseed, Rock Bass.

Secondary - Smallmouth Bass, Northern Pike, Perch, Cisco.

Limited - Largemouth Bass.

COMMENT - Walleye are present in good numbers and display good reproduction. The muskie population is excellent in both numbers and size of fish available. Northern pike numbers seem to be increasing.

LAKE MANAGEMENT

Lake Investigation Data - A recent spring fyke net survey was conducted to evaluate the walleye population. The results of this study showed a good density of 5.1 fish per acre and an estimated total population of 4,719 adult fish.

BIG MUSKELLUNGE LAKE FYKE NET SUMMARY		
SPECIES	SIZE RANGE	NUMBER
Walleye	8.5" - 11.9"	532
Walleye	12.0" - 14.9"	857
Walleye	15.0" - 29.9"	196

Stocking

BIG MUSKELLUNGE LAKE STOCKING SUMMARY			
YEAR	SPECIES	NUMBER	SIZE
1980	Muskie	1,000	8"
1981	Walleye	39,950	Fingerling
1982	Muskie	1,800	3"
1983	Walleye	27,000	3"
1985	Muskie (Private)	150	9"
1986	Muskie	1,800	8"
1987	Muskie (Private)	1,065	9" - 12"
	Muskie	16,200	Fry
1988	Muskie	1,800	Fingerling
1990	Muskie	1,740	Fingerling

BIG MUSKELLUNGE LAKE

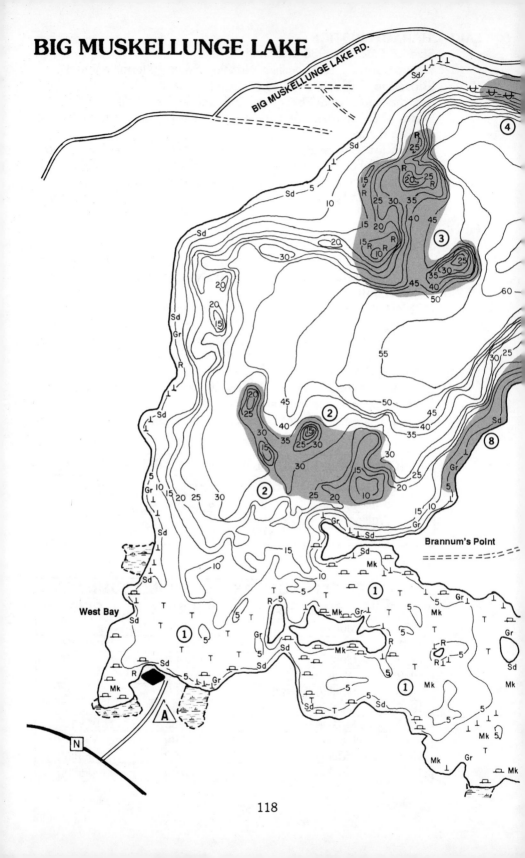

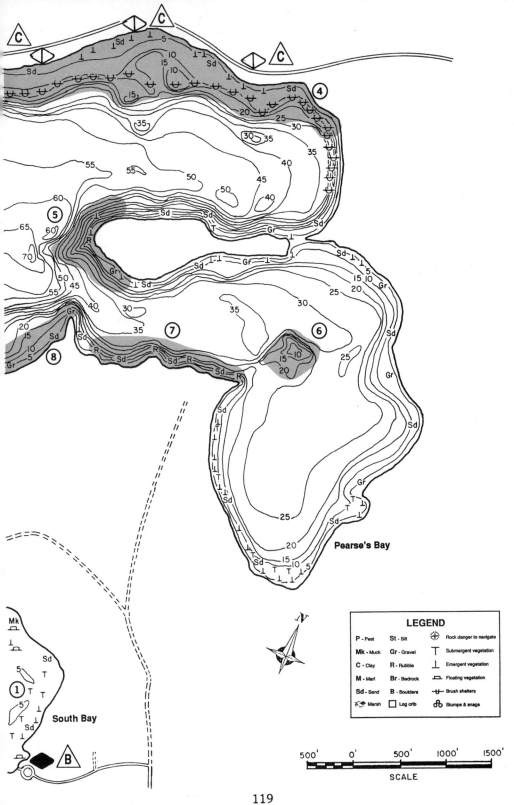

Pearse's Bay

South Bay

LEGEND

P - Peat   St - Silt   Rock danger to navigate

Mk - Muck   Gr - Gravel   Submergent vegetation

C - Clay   R - Rubble   Emergent vegetation

M - Marl   Br - Bedrock   Floating vegetation

Sd - Sand   B - Boulders   Brush shelters

Marsh   Log crib   Stumps & snags

SCALE

500'   0'   500'   1000'   1500'

Treatment - Thirty brush shelters have been placed in the 10- to 15-foot depths on the north and northeast shoreline. Despite their age, they still provide cover.

LAKE SURVEY MAP - Fishing Areas Shaded

Area (1) Emergent, submergent and floating vegetation is common in West and South Bays. Muskie, largemouth bass and panfish are available. Work the edge of the weeds during the ice fishing season for walleye. Many anglers prefer to fish West Bay after dark.

Area (2) Fish the sharp drops, humps and submerged points during summer and fall for deep-water walleye and muskie. Use a depthfinder to locate the most productive areas.

Area (3) A series of deep-water rock bars on the north shoreline provides exceptional summer and fall muskie and walleye fishing. Vertical jig the edges of the deeper structure, and use slip bobber rigs on the shallow rock humps for walleye. Deep-running crankbaits and jerkbaits are recommended for muskie.

Area (4) Work the 10- to 13-foot depths along the north shoreline with deep-diving crankbaits for smallmouth bass and walleye. The old log cribs provide some of the best muskie action on the lake. Smallmouth and walleye can also be found near these structures.

Area (5) The west shoreline of the island has a long point that drops into deep water. Backtroll the edges of this point for walleye, smallmouth bass and muskie.

Area (6) This sunken island in Pearses Bay is popular for muskie and smallmouth bass. Twitch Rapalas over the shallow portion of the bar during low light periods for bass.

Area (7) Work small crayfish-colored crankbaits along this rocky shoreline for smallmouth bass. Cast parallel to the drop-off for best results.

Area (8) Muskie and walleye use the submerged logs along this shoreline. Jerkbaits and in-line spinners are effective for muskie. Fish the edges of the logs with slip bobber rigs for walleye.

FISHING TIPS - Rock bars, sunken islands, submerged logs and shoreline drop-offs attract a majority of the fish. A good depthfinder is valuable for locating and working these areas.

Crankbaits are recommended for shoreline muskie, especially for working the sharp drop-offs, cribs and submerged logs. Bucktails or surface lures are suggested for the cabbage of South or West Bay.

Walleye relate to the edge of the cabbage beds in early spring and from late fall through winter. Fish the sharp drops on the deep side of the reefs for larger walleye, especially from midsummer to October.

CONCLUSION - Big Muskellunge Lake offers good fishing for walleye and muskie. Muskie fishing is better-than-average as decent numbers of fish up to 40 inches are present, and the lake has potential to produce a trophy.

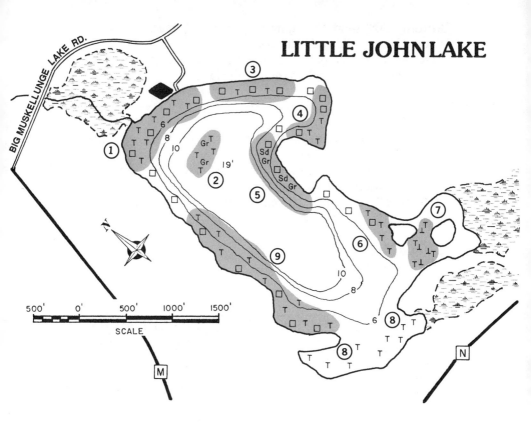

LITTLE JOHN LAKE

LOCATION - In the south central part of the area, just north of Highway N and just east of Highway M.

ACCESS - Type I (Public): On the north end of the lake; take Big Muskellunge Lake Road east off Highway M for 0.5 mile to the marked boat landing road. At the end of this state forest road is a paved parking area and concrete ramp. Drinking water is also available.

RELATED SERVICES
    Boat Rentals - Yes.
    Resorts - None.
    Campgrounds - None.

LAKE CHARACTERISTICS
    Size and Depth - 166 acres and 19 feet.
    Water Source - Spring-fed lake: An outlet on the northwest end to Allequash Creek.
    Shoreline - 90% state-owned, except for the southwest corner.

Bottom - 70% sand, 20% gravel, 5% rock, 5% muck.

Water - Very fertile and quite clear.

Vegetation - Submergent weedbeds are present along the shoreline zone and throughout the southern end of the lake.

FISHERY

SPECIES

Primary - Muskie, Walleye, Perch, Rock Bass, Pumpkinseed, Sucker.

Secondary - Largemouth Bass, Northern Pike, Crappie, Bluegill.

Limited - Smallmouth Bass, Burbot.

COMMENT - Generally, gamefish populations are in good shape with above-average growth rates.

LAKE MANAGEMENT

Lake Investigation Data - None.

Stocking

LITTLE JOHN LAKE STOCKING SUMMARY			
YEAR	SPECIES	NUMBER	SIZE
1983	Walleye	8,000	3"
1984	Walleye	8,000	3"
1985	Muskie	300	Fingerling
1988	Muskie	200	Fingerling
1990	Muskie	114	Fingerling

Treatment - Forty-one log cribs were installed in 1967 around the entire shoreline except for the southwest and southeast bays.

LAKE SURVEY MAP - Fishing Areas Shaded

Area (1) Work the abundant weed cover for northern pike, muskie, and an occasional largemouth bass. The warmer water near the outlet provides early muskie action from May into June.

Area (2) Walleye and muskie inhabit this gravel bar for much of the season. Backtroll the edge of the sandgrass from the outlet creek south toward the middle of the lake.

Area (3) This steep shoreline drop-off offers walleye fishing. Remember that the presence of the old cribs helps to concentrate forage. Muskie and bass are a distinct possibility.

Area (4) Cribs and submerged weeds provide cover for largemouth bass and panfish. Flip the inside and outside weed edges with Texas-rigged plastic worms.

Area (5) Walleye and smallmouth are found on this sand/gravel bar on the east shore. Cast deep-diving crankbaits along the drop-off and over the cribs.

Area (6) Backtroll the deep weed edge off the north island for walleye and perhaps a muskie.

Area (7) Largemouth bass, muskie and walleye are attracted to the abundant emergent and submergent vegetation west of the island.

Area (8) The weedy southwest bay is a popular location for bass and pike anglers. Work the deep weed edge for active fish.

Area (9) The west shoreline offers typical Little John Lake structure - scattered weedbeds, old cribs, and nice drop-offs. Muskie, walleye and bass are all possibilities.

FISHING TIPS - Fishing this productive lake is not difficult because shoreline structure attracts fish and provides easy casting targets. Work the shoreline weedbeds and old cribs for muskie, largemouth bass, walleye and panfish. It is important to cast parallel to the deep weed edges. Submerged weed points, inside turns and open areas in the weeds often concentrate fish. Weed walleye techniques, especially slip bobber rigging, produce in summer. In early spring, concentrate on gravel drop-offs.

CONCLUSION - Despite the relatively small size, Little John Lake offers a surprising fishery in both diversity and quality. This lake definitely belongs on your list.

LITTLE JOHN JR. LAKE

LOCATION - In the southeast part of the area, just south of Highway N and east of Highway M.

ACCESS - Type III: On the west side of the lake at the north bay; from Highway N, turn south on Highland Trail for 0.1 mile. Then turn east a short distance on the unmarked access road to the landing. There is a short carry-in down a steep trail to a beach landing.

SPECIAL FEATURES - Motors are prohibited.

LAKE CHARACTERISTICS
    Size and Depth - 21 acres and 30 feet.
    Water Source - Seepage lake: No inlet or outlet.
    Shoreline - 100% state-owned.
    Bottom - Sand with gravel and some muck and rock.
    Water - Highly infertile and quite clear. Good dissolved oxygen levels to depths of 15 feet.
    Vegetation - Limited to a narrow shoreline zone. Lily pads are present.

FISHERY
    SPECIES - Brown Trout, Brook Trout.
    COMMENT - Management focuses on brown trout due to inadequate

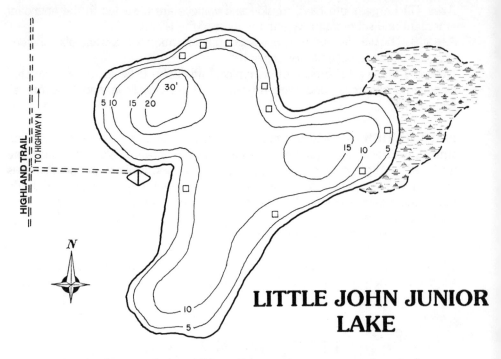

LITTLE JOHN JUNIOR LAKE

dissolved oxygen below 15 feet. Brown trout are more tolerant of warmer water temperatures. A lack of forage apparently limits growth.

LAKE MANAGEMENT

Lake Investigation Data - None recently.

Stocking

LITTLE JOHN Jr. LAKE STOCKING SUMMARY			
YEAR	SPECIES	NUMBER	SIZE
1982	Brown Trout	2,000	Yearling
1983	Brook Trout	2,000	Yearling
1984	Brook Trout	1,500	Yearling
1985	Brook Trout	1,000	Yearling
	Brown Trout	1,000	Yearling
1986	Brook Trout	1,000	Yearling
	Brown Trout	1,000	Yearling
1987	Brook Trout	1,000	Yearling
	Brown Trout	1,000	Yearling
1988	Brown Trout	2,000	Yearling
1989	Brown Trout	2,000	Yearling
1990	Brown Trout	2,000	Yearling

Treatment - Nine log cribs were installed in 1967.

FISHING TIPS - The entire lake averages 10 to 15 feet except for a deep hole in the northwest bay. Try working your lures in the vicinity of the old crib.

Fishing in early morning or late evening hours is always recommended. Dry flies, wet flies, nymph imitations and streamers are good offerings. Look for feeding fish whenever a hatch is occurring.

CONCLUSION - This lake can provide a quality fishing experience for brown trout and perhaps a few remnant brook trout. Expect moderate fishing pressure.

CRYSTAL LAKE

LOCATION - In the southeast part of the area, north of Highway N and south of Big Muskellunge Lake.

ACCESS - Type I (Public): On the south side of the lake, at the state campground just north of Highway N. This campground entrance is well-marked on Highway N.

RELATED SERVICES
>**Boat Rentals** - None.
>**Resorts** - None.
>**Campgrounds** - Yes, a state-owned facility.
>**Public Parks** - Yes, a large picnic area.

SPECIAL FEATURES - Attractive public use facilities including a large, sand beach. No motors allowed.

LAKE CHARACTERISTICS
>**Size and Depth** - 88 acres and 67 feet.
>**Water Source** - Seepage lake: No inlet or outlet.
>**Shoreline** - 100% state-owned. Entirely upland.
>**Bottom** - Primarily sand with some gravel.
>**Water** - Extremely infertile and exceptionally clear. Good oxygen levels to 54 feet deep.
>**Vegetation** - Extremely limited and confined to the shoreline.

FISHERY
>**SPECIES** - Lake Trout, Smallmouth Bass, Largemouth Bass, Perch, Bluegill, Rock Bass, Pumpkinseed, Bullhead, Smelt.
>**COMMENT** - A remnant lake trout population is present. Both gamefish and panfish numbers are relatively low and show below average growth rates.

CRYSTAL LAKE

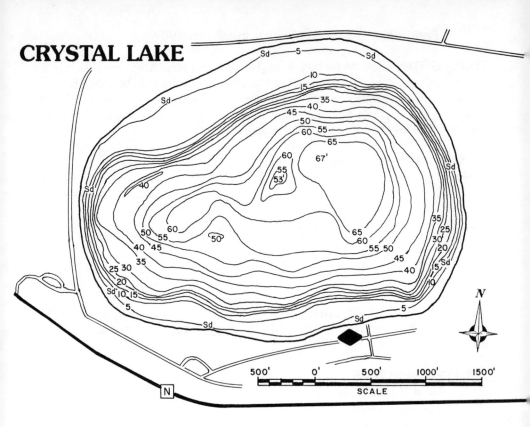

LAKE MANAGEMENT
Lake Investigation Data - None recently.
Stocking - None recently.

CONCLUSION - Crystal Lake is popular during the summer months for swimming, camping and picnicking.

LAKE 30-16 (UNNAMED)

LOCATION - In the south central part of the area, just east of Highway M, south of Highway N, and north of Mann Lake.

ACCESS - Type III: On the southwest end of the lake; from Highway M, go east on Mann Lake Lane for about ½ mile to an old logging trail. Turn north a short distance to the landing. (See the Mann Lake map).

LAKE CHARACTERISTICS
Size and Depth - 8 acres and 25 feet.
Water Source - Seepage lake: No inlet or outlet.

Shoreline - 100% state-owned, 100% wetland.
Bottom - Mostly muck with some sand.
Water - Extremely infertile and a bit murky.
Vegetation - Limited due to the rapid shoreline drop-off.

FISHERY
SPECIES - Largemouth Bass, Perch.
COMMENT - Perch totally dominate the fishery of this pothole lake. A few bass in the 13- to 15-inch range have been reported.

LAKE MANAGEMENT
Lake Investigation Data - None recently.
Stocking - None.

CONCLUSION - Apparently, the influence of good oxygen levels has meant that a small number of bass do achieve moderate size. However, the lake's ability to sustain any number of quality fish is minimal because of the overabundant perch.

MANN LAKE

LOCATION - In the south central part of the area, just east of Highway M and south of Highway N.

ACCESS - Type I: On the west end of the lake; take Mann Lake Lane 200 feet east from Highway M to a gravel road. Go south for 0.2 mile to the state forest access. This unimproved access has a beach landing and room to park several vehicles.

RELATED SERVICES
Boat Rentals - Yes.
Resorts - Yes.
Campgrounds - None.

SPECIAL FEATURES - Water levels have been adjusted in an attempt to eliminate serious winterkill problems.

LAKE CHARACTERISTICS
Size and Depth - 261 acres and 18 feet.
Water Source - Spring-fed lake: The Mann Creek outlet on the west end flows to Trout Lake. There is a water level control dam at the outlet.
Shoreline - 80% state-owned, except for the northwest portion and a 2,000-foot section along the south shore. Primarily upland.
Bottom - 40% muck, 30% sand, 30% gravel.
Water - Exceptionally fertile and a little murky. There is a history of winterkill.

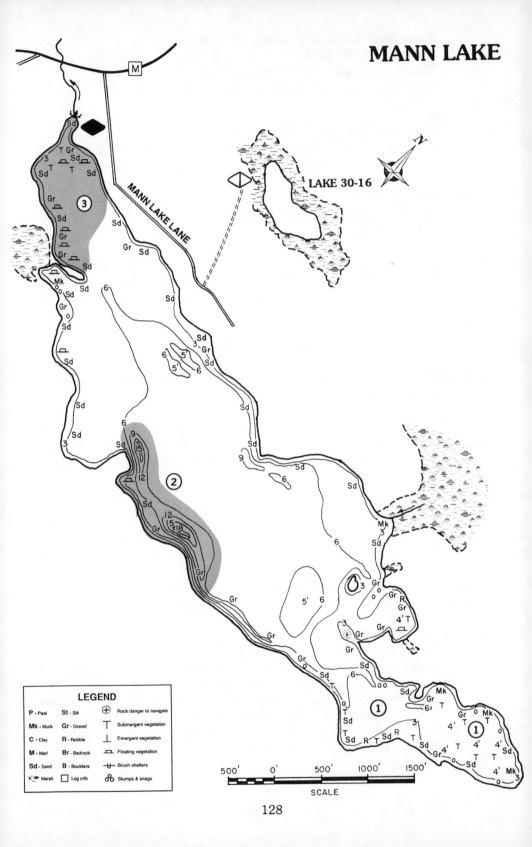

MANN LAKE

LAKE 30-16

MANN LAKE LANE

LEGEND

P - Peat	**St** - Silt	Rock danger to navigate
Mk - Muck	**Gr** - Gravel	Submergent vegetation
C - Clay	**R** - Rubble	Emergent vegetation
M - Marl	**Br** - Bedrock	Floating vegetation
Sd - Sand	**B** - Boulders	Brush shelters
Marsh	Log crib	Stumps & snags

SCALE

500'   0'   500'   1000'   1500'

128

Vegetation - Abundant weed growth, including emergent, submergent and floating varieties.

FISHERY
SPECIES
Primary - Northern Pike, Perch, Sucker.
Secondary - Pumpkinseed.
Limited - Muskie, Walleye, Largemouth Bass, Rock Bass, Crappie, Bluegill.

COMMENT - Northern pike and perch are common because they can withstand the effects of low oxygen levels. In recent years, the water control structure has lowered water levels during winter to aleviate the oxygen shortage. However, during the average winter, levels remain very low - usually less than 2.0 ppm.

Many northern pike between 14 and 18 inches present, along with a few larger fish.

LAKE MANAGEMENT
Lake Investigation Data - None recently.
Stocking

MANN LAKE STOCKING SUMMARY			
YEAR	SPECIES	NUMBER	SIZE
1989	Bluegill	330	3"
	Northern Pike	93	10"
1990	Largemouth Bass	200	Yearling
	Bluegill	2,950	Adult

LAKE SURVEY MAP - Fishing Areas Shaded
Area (1) Work the shallow submergent weed growth with in-line spinners, spinnerbaits, or floating balsa lures for northern pike. Concentrate on the deepest weedlines for bigger fish.
Area (2) The two deepest holes in the lake can offer decent perch fishing, especially in fall.
Area (3) Northern pike are plentiful in the weedy western end of the lake.

FISHING TIPS - Northern pike provide action year-round. A selection of in-line spinners, spinnerbaits, and floating balsa minnows all take fish. Look for deeper weed edges and channels to produce the best action. Rapala-type minnows "twitched" slowly over the weed tops are always a good bet.

CONCLUSION - While northern pike are available in large numbers, Mann Lake offers fun fishing for quantity not quality.

FIREFLY LAKE

FIREFLY LAKE (WEBER LAKE)

LOCATION - In the southeast portion of the area, south of Highway N, and east of Highway M.

ACCESS - Type IV: On the west side of the lake; from Highway N, drive south on Highland Trail for 0.7 mile to the landing. Parking and a short carry-in to a beach landing are provided.

RELATED SERVICES
    Boat Rentals - None.
    Resorts - None.
    Campgrounds - Yes, a large state campground on the north shore.
    Public Parks - Yes, part of the campground.

SPECIAL FEATURES - Motors and live bait are prohibited. Firefly is one of the clearest lakes in Wisconsin.

LAKE CHARACTERISTICS
    Size and Depth - 27 acres and 46 feet.

Water Source - Seepage lake: No inlet or outlet.

Shoreline - 100% state-owned. Mostly upland.

Bottom - Almost entirely sand with some gravel.

Water - Very infertile and extremely clear. Good oxygen levels are present at all depths.

Vegetation - Very scarce.

FISHERY

SPECIES - Brook Trout, Brown Trout, Rainbow Trout, Perch, Rock Bass, Pumpkinseed.

COMMENT - State management focuses on a trout fishery, including a recent shift to brown trout.

LAKE MANAGEMENT

Lake Investigation Data - None recently.

Stocking - Firefly has been stocked with trout since 1942.

Treatment - In 1967, 32 fish cribs were installed around the shoreline. They are spaced in regular intervals, except for the south bay.

FISHING TIPS - Firefly is very infertile and totally without structure. Trout fishermen are urged to work the cribs, presenting dry or wet flies, and small spinners or spoons.

CONCLUSION - Firefly Lake is a beautiful little lake, offering swimming, canoeing, camping and trout fishing.

EMERALD LAKE (RUTH LAKE)

LOCATION - In the southeast part of the area, south of Highway N, and east of Highways M and 51.

ACCESS - Type III: On the northeast end of the lake; from Highway N, proceed south on Highland Trail for 0.7 mile to the Firefly Lake landing. Turn right on a logging road and stay on this main trail for 0.8 mile to an intersection with another logging road. Turn right and proceed 0.2 mile to the access on the right. It is a rather steep walk-in to the bog-lined shore. (Note: In dry weather, these logging roads are passable for most vehicles.)

SPECIAL FEATURES - Motors are prohibited. Emerald has been classified by the DNR as an experimental lake.

LAKE CHARACTERISTICS

Size and Depth - 27 acres and 22 feet.

Water Source - Seepage lake: No inlet or outlet.

EMERALD LAKE

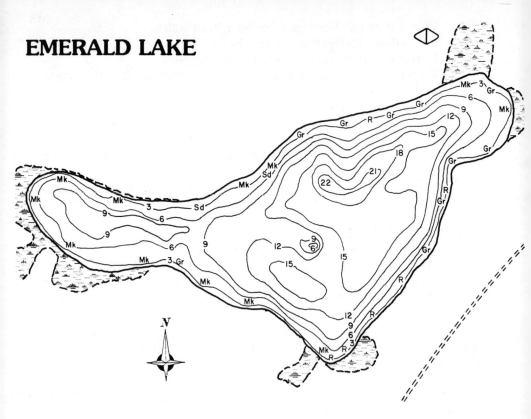

Shoreline - 100% state-owned.

Bottom - Mostly muck with some sand and gravel.

Water - Extremely infertile and quite clear. Good dissolved oxygen is present down to 12 feet.

Vegetation - Limited to a narrow fringe of bog that encircles most of the shoreline.

FISHERY

SPECIES - Largemouth Bass, Bluegill.

COMMENT - Emerald is being managed as a bluegill and largemouth bass fishery.

LAKE MANAGEMENT

Lake Investigation Data - None recently.

Stocking - In 1990, 250 ten-inch largemouth bass were stocked.

Treatment - Chemical treatment to remove stunted bluegill was conducted in 1985. Following treatment (1986 and 1987), the lake was restocked with female bluegill.

CONCLUSION - Look for a largemouth bass and bluegill fishery if the bluegill experiment produces the desired results.

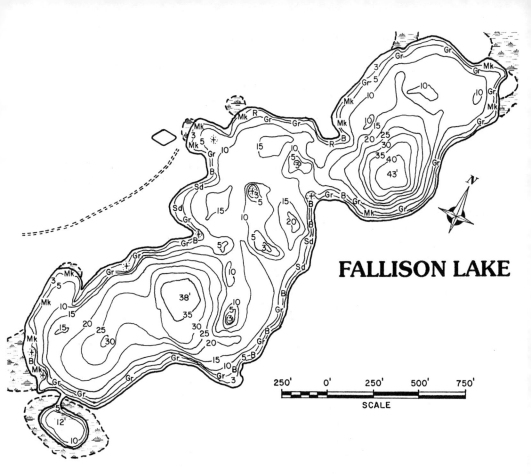

FALLISON LAKE

LOCATION - In the southeast part of the area, south of Highway N and east of Highway M, immediately below Crystal Lake.

ACCESS - Type IV (Public): On the west side of the lake: from Highway N, turn south on Highland Trail Road for 0.7 mile to the Firefly Lake landing. Turn right on a logging trail for 0.6 mile. The road is blocked at this point to automobile traffic. Continue for 0.2 mile to an intersection with another trail. Turn right and go past Emerald Lake a total of 0.4 mile to a fork in the trail. Stay left for the last 0.2 mile to the short easy carry-in to the lake.

SPECIAL FEATURES - Motors are prohibited. A nature trail starts on Highway N and circles the lake.

LAKE CHARACTERISTICS
    Size and Depth - 52 acres and 43 feet.

Water Source - Seepage lake: No inlet or outlet.
Shoreline - 100% state-owned.
Bottom - Mostly sand, with gravel, rock and muck.
Water - Exceptionally infertile and very clear.
Vegetation - Very few weeds are present.

FISHERY

SPECIES - Brook Trout, Rainbow Trout.
COMMENT - The lake has been managed for trout since 1978. Brook trout provide most of the action. Fish up to 17 inches have been taken.

LAKE MANAGEMENT

Lake Investigation Data - None recently.
Stocking

FALLISON LAKE STOCKING SUMMARY			
YEAR	SPECIES	NUMBER	SIZE
1984	Rainbow Trout	5,000	Fingerling
	Brook Trout	5,000	Fingerling
1985	Rainbow Trout	5,000	Fingerling
	Brook Trout	5,000	Fingerling
1986	Rainbow Trout	5,000	FIngerling
	Brook Trout	5,000	Fingerling
1987	Rainbow Trout	5,000	Adult
	Brook Trout	5,000	Adult
1988	Rainbow Trout	5,000	5"
	Brook Trout	5,000	5"
1989	Brook Trout	5,000	5"

CONCLUSION - This stocked trout fishery can offer decent action in a wilderness setting.

WILDWOOD LAKE

LOCATION - In the southeast part of the area, south of Highway N and east of Highway 51.

ACCESS - Type IV: On the west end of the lake; from Highway N, proceed south on Highland Trail for 0.7 mile to the Firefly Lake landing. Turn right on a logging road, and stay on this main trail for 0.6 mile. The road is blocked at this point to automobile traffic. Proceed 0.2 mile to an intersection with another logging road. Turn right and go past Emerald Lake, a total of 0.4 mile to a fork in the road. Turn to the right for 300 feet to another fork; then stay to the right for 0.5 mile to an easy carry-in to the lake.

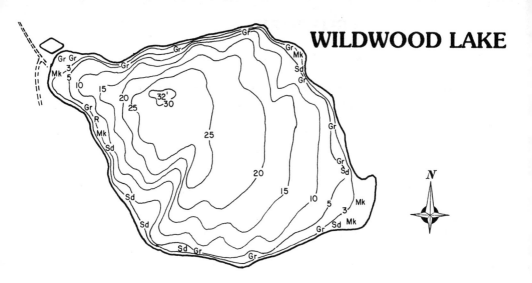

WILDWOOD LAKE

SPECIAL FEATURES - No motors allowed. Only artificial flies and lures may be used.

LAKE CHARACTERISTICS
    Size and Depth - 16 acres and 31 feet.
    Water Source - Seepage lake: No inlet or outlet.
    Shoreline - 100% state-owned.
    Bottom - Mostly sand, with some muck and gravel.
    Water - Exceptionally infertile and very clear.
    Vegetation - Both emergent and submergent types are available on the shoreline.

FISHERY
    SPECIES - Brown Trout.
    COMMENT - After chemical treatment in 1981 to remove the stunted bluegill population, brown trout were stocked the following year.

LAKE MANAGEMENT
    Lake Investigation Data - A recent fyke net survey reported successful carry-over of brown trout. Seventy-eight trout, ranging from 11½ to 16½ inches were surveyed. The state has reported that brown trout can survive in a soft-water lake.

    Stocking - Approximately 2,000 brown trout fingerling are planted each year.

CONCLUSION - A quality brown trout fishery is available.

GLOSSARY

BIOMASS - A biological term to describe the entire amount of fish of all species in any given lake.

BREAKLINE - A length or distance along a lake's bottom where the drop off changes to a steeper gradient. Often this occurs at a specific depth of water.

EDGE - The border or fringe of any fish-holding habitat-including weeds, wood, brush, rock breakline, etc. Traditionally a good place to fish.

FERTILITY - The biological productivity of the water in a lake. A high fertility usually results in a quality fishery due to a well-developed food chain. However, it can also lead to overly dense vegetation and algae blooms. A lake with extremely low fertility often has stunted fish populations.

FISHERY - All the species of fish that inhabit a lake.

GAMEFISH - The group of fish sought by anglers, including muskie, northern pike, walleye, largemouth bass, smallmouth bass and trout.

HABITAT - A region to which fish relate and can often be found. Usually associated with some form of structure - bottom, weeds, wood, etc. Providing either cover and/or food.

LAKE TYPES

    SPRING - Always a substantial outlet, but rarely an inlet. Most of the water supply comes from groundwater. Often the most fertile type of lake.

    DRAINAGE - Has at least one inlet and an outlet. Water supply comes from stream drainage and direct run-off. Usually very fertile with a diversified and quality fishery.

    DRAINED - Has a "small flow" outlet, but rarely an inlet. Water supply comes from groundwater sources. Usually moderately infertile with bass and panfish the main fishery.

    SEEPAGE - No inlet or outlet (landlocked). Water supply comes from groundwater sources. Usually very infertile with only bass and panfish populations. An exception would be a large seepage lake with a stocked fishery.

LITTORAL ZONE - The shore area of the lake. Usually out to the 5-foot depth or the outside edge of the shoreline weeds. This zone is referred to in the discussion of bottom materials.

PANFISH - The group of fish sought by anglers, including perch, bluegill, crappie, rock bass, pumpkinseed and bullhead.

STRUCTURE - A distinguishing break or change on the bottom of the lake that separates it from the surrounding bottom.

STUNTED PANFISH - A panfish population that does not maintain an average rate of growth. These populations are associated with lakes of low fertility, where food supplies are inadequate.

THERMOCLINE - A layer of reasonably well-oxygenated summer lake water that displays a rapid drop in temperature from top to bottom. This water will range from 45 to 65 degrees Fahrenheit, and will hold fish preferring cooler water. This layer prevents the wind from circulating warmer surface water into the colder bottom layers.

YEAR CLASS - The group of any particular species of fish produced in any given year.

TIPS ON RELEASING FISH

1. After the decision is made to release a fish, do not play it to a "state of exhaustion." If you plan to release a fish try to keep the time from hooksetting to release at a minimum.

2. If at all possible, do not remove your fish from water, release it in the water where its body is supported.

3. Remove hooks with long-nosed pliers. If hook removal is difficult and may cause injury to the fish, cut the hook off with wire cutters or else cut the line. Do not attempt to remove deeply embedded hooks from fish.

4. Care should be taken not to remove the fish's protective body mucous.

5. A dry hand, contrary to popular opinion, reduces the amount of pressure required to restrain the fish and therefore decreases the chance of internal injury. If at all possible, avoid handling the fish. A landing net can save a large fish from injury and help restrain the fish while removing the hook.

6. When landing a fish, use a net rather than a gaff. If you decide to net your fish, be careful so it doesn't thrash around in the boat and injure itself. If hook removal is done inside the boat, lay your fish on a wet, soft surface, like a wet gunny sack. Don't hold the fish up when removing the hook.

7. With a squirming, hard to handle fish the natural reaction is to slide your hand forward until pressure is placed on the gill covers. Do not hold a fish by the gill covers, as undue force may result in injury to the gills. Remember, never hold a fish by the eye socket or gills.

8. Hold your unhooked fish horizontally and righted in the water with both hands - one supporting the belly and the other holding near the tail. If the gill covers are not moving, gently move the fish back and forth in the water to facilitate breathing. Hold your fish until it can remain in an upright position and swim away by itself.

9. If the fish must be out of the water for any length of time, cover the head with a wet cloth (i.e., gunny sack) to help prevent drying of the eyes and gills.

10. Never release a large fish, such as muskie, northern, or bass over deep water. An exhausted fish is incapable of adjusting to the pressure of deep water.

11. A quick and accurate method of measuring fish is marking foot increments on the side of the boat or by taking a wooden ruler and laying it next to the fish in the water.

12. Do not take picture of your fish hanging from a scale, stringer, or being held by the gill covers if you intend to release it. This will put unnecessary strain on the delicate supportive and connective tissues between the head and body, as well as the vertebrae.

Tips courtesy of Muskies. Inc.

Fishing Hot Spots
Supports
Catch and Release

Keeping Up-to-Date With
Help From Our Friends -

This book was published to help anglers decide where to fish. We have stressed factual, organized data on the lakes of the Boulder Junction area . . . information that you will find most important in enjoying your time on the water.

Some of the material is continuously subject to change by the forces of nature or man. As you come across these discrepancies in the book, please take a moment to let us know of your findings.

Much of the information presented in this book came from anglers like you. If when you are in the Boulder Junction area you find a new access, an access improvement, a service facility, a hot spot or a new fishing pattern, please let us know.

Drop us a line at *Fishing Hot Spots*, 1999 River Street, P.O. Box 1167, Rhinelander, WI 54501. The more specific your comments, the better. Thank You and good fishin'.

Bob Knops
President

NOTES:

THE DIFFERENCE BETWEEN THE FISHING PRO AND NOVICE?...

KNOWLEDGE!

Fishing Hot Spots®
PUBLICATIONS

Now YOU can join the experts in catching limits of fish!

The **Fishing Hot Spots** series of publications will provide you with the knowledge of **where** to catch fish. Factual and up-to-date research!

Each book or Lake Map/Report includes:
- Complete **Lake Maps** marked with proven **"hot spots"**
- Hard-to-find **stocking reports**
- Lake characteristics including bottom composition, fertility and vegetation.
- Complete **lake study reports** including test netting results
- Lake access locations
- Results of interviews with those who fish and manage the lakes.
- Availability of resorts, campgrounds, bait shops and much, much more.

"I have bought several of your books, and I must say they've helped my fishing immensely. I no longer fumble my way around on a new lake. Your books helped me to my largest muskie to date, a beautiful 30 pounder. So keep up the great work."
ROD K., Freeport, IL

"...thanks to your books I have caught many species of fish along with (some) very enjoyable times on these lakes. My wife and I were catching nice size bluegill while other people were watching their bobbers float."
JERRY A., Milwaukee, WI

"...Information is the anglers' answer to both location and presentation patterns. The FISHING HOT SPOTS organization puts out quality publications that fill the anglers' needs for locating hot spots to fish.
BABE WINKELMAN, BWP

For A Free Catalog Write Fishing Hot Spots, 1999 River Street, Rhinelander, WI 54501
Or Call (715) 369-5555